PAUL BRUNSON

NOT
AFRAID
TO
W RK

Practical Advice for
the Young **Electrician**

Copyright © 2024 by Paul Brunson

All rights reserved. No part of this book may be reproduced, stored in a retrieval system, or used in any manner without the prior written permission of the copyright owner except for the use of brief quotations in book review.

To request permissions, contact the publisher
BE Publishing at paul@brunsonelectric.com.

Paperback ISBN: 979-8-218-35597-5
eBook ISBN: 979-8-218-35598-2

Paperback edition: January 2024

Book design by Silke Spingies

Printed in the United States of America

Dedicated to my beautiful wife Kelly, who was the one that pushed me to write this book. Also, to my son John, you're the future...no pressure!

This book is for all the hardworking young people out there that are looking for something constructive to put their energy into.

Special thanks to my editor Lia Ottaviano.

Endorsements

" Paul Brunson's *Not Afraid to Work: Practical Advice for Young Electrician*, is the best step-by step guide for those considering a successful career as an electrician. It is a candid presentation of the pros and cons written from his own experiences and his extraordinarily successful career as a professional electrician.

Paul has been a valuable mentor to countless young electricians throughout the years. By acquiring this book readers are really engaging Paul as their personal mentor. His straightforward writing style makes the reader feel that he wrote this book just for you.

I recommend everyone interested in a career as a professional electrician to get, *Not Afraid to Work: Practical Advice for Young Electrician*. It will be invaluable to your decision to enter the trade and a lifelong roadmap to a successful career."

Don Wetmore,
The Tradesman's Business Coach Author,
The Productivity Handbook

> Paul Brunson's book is an invaluable tool for aspiring electricians. With a diverse background in the military, industrial, commercial, and residential sectors his wealth of experience spans every discipline of the trade. He imparts invaluable technical knowledge and, more importantly, offers crucial insights into cultivating the right mindset to succeed. Not only as an electrician, but as a professional. A must-read for anyone beginning their journey into this dynamic field."

Ian Stewart,
Master Electrician/Electrical Contractor

> This book offers a guide to help people new to the trade or considering an apprenticeship. Using real-life stories and his experience, Paul brings an electrician's career to life, showing the benefits of choosing a career as an electrician. You can get a first-hand look at overcoming the pitfalls and finding opportunities to succeed."

Chad C. Betz,
Business Coach, Author and Speaker

Contents

Introduction

The Tools Of The Trade   9

Chapter 1

Why Choose Electrical Over College?
Making The Case For The Trades   19

Chapter 2

The Misconceptions Of The "Back Up Plan"   31

Chapter 3

Landing Your First Job As An Apprentice   49

Chapter 4

Mastering Soft Skills   57

Chapter 5

The Down And Dirty Of Electrical Work   67

Chapter 6

The Electrical Trade As A Path To Entrepreneurship   75

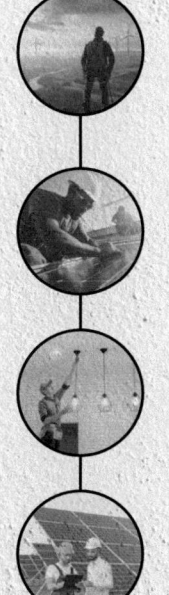

Chapter 7

Creating Your Own Luck (The Tale Of Two Electricians)   89

Chapter 8

Theory Vs. Practice: The Value Of Hands-On Experience   111

Chapter 9

Side Jobs: A Dirty Word   121

Chapter 10

Staying Organized And Knowing What To Expect   127

Conclusion

Putting It All Together   139

Apprentice Task Checklist   143
Apprenticeship Skill List   155
Understanding Wiring Diagrams   163
50 Tips For Apprentices   167
General Knowledge Check   175
Key Terms   181

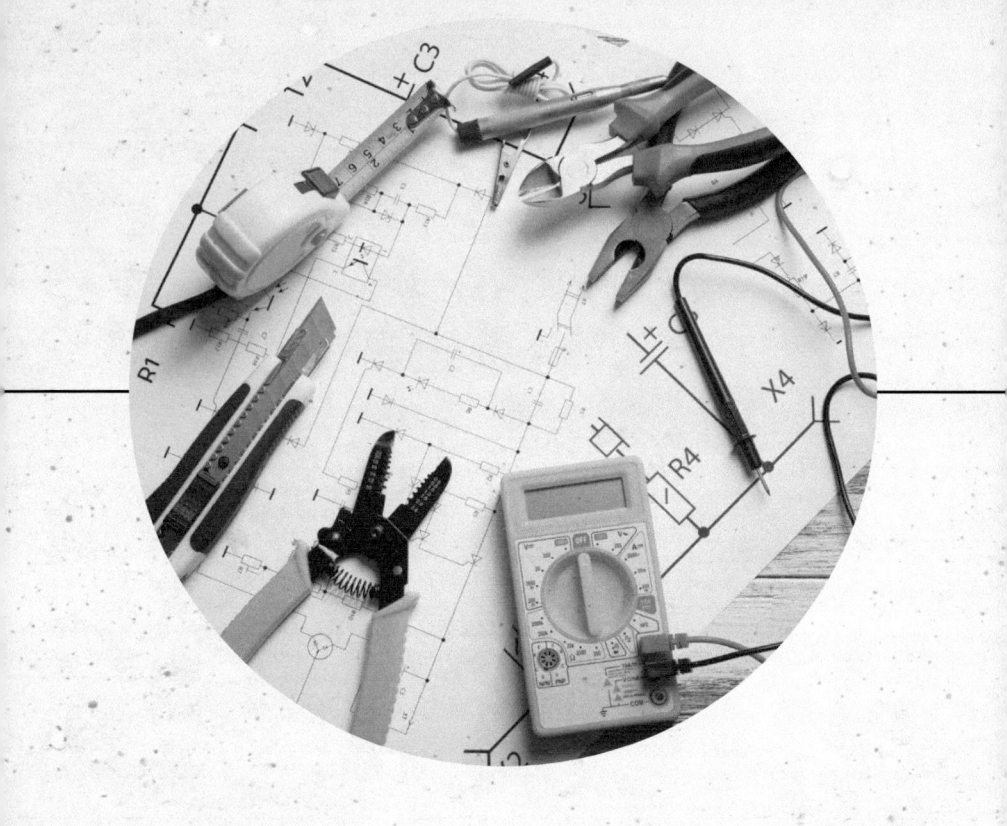

Introduction

The Tools Of The Trade

G etting into the electrical trade was one of the best decisions I've ever made. It has afforded me some amazing opportunities and has thrown many challenges my way. It's also allowed me to grow professionally and personally, doing honest, hard work that I can be proud of. I've served as a helper, an apprentice, a journeyman, a foreman, an estimator, a project manager, and an electrical contractor. I even had the opportunity to serve in the United States Air Force, working on aircraft electrical systems. With eighteen years of experience in this trade already behind me, I feel like I'm just getting started. I'm grateful for the opportunities this industry **constantly throws** my way and look forward to pursuing new challenges as I go.

I was lucky enough to fall into the trade somewhat by accident. Like many high school seniors, I had no clue what I wanted to spend my life doing. I knew I liked hard work.

At least, I certainly knew I wasn't afraid of it. I also enjoyed hands-on work over paperwork or computers. I was a decent student but felt like a white-collar job might not be active enough. I'd always been attracted to mechanical things, and I'd also been into cars and aircraft. I thought about becoming a machinist or an aviation mechanic.

As I pondered the trajectory of my life, I worked a few odd jobs my senior year, including landscaping and bagging groceries. Although I didn't know it at the time, right after I got out of high school, I was about to catch my lucky break. I found a summer job through a family friend at a two-way radio shop. This company sold and repaired handheld, two-way radios. The busy sales and repair departments had an antiquated customer database system that was still written on index cards. They needed someone they didn't have to pay much to file their paperwork and get their customer files into an electronic database. It seemed like a good three-month gig to make some money and plan my next move. At this point, I still hadn't ruled out college. This opportunity also bought me time to research schools while I made a few bucks.

I'd made it about three weeks into my new gig, and things were moving along fine. The work was very tedious, boring, and sedentary, but I was happy to have a job and proud to be earning a paycheck, and that left bagging groceries in the dust. One morning, one of the bosses came out to the back of the office where I was clicking away on a keyboard, entering hundreds of thousands of lines of customer contact information into a database. "Hey kid, you know how to work with tools?" I didn't know what he meant specifically, and I didn't know if my limited experience would even scratch the surface of what they were looking for. I knew I had some basic mechanical ability, but I had absolutely no practical skills. I didn't know what to say, but I recognized an opportunity when I saw one, so my "fake it 'til you make it" instinct kicked right in.

"Yeah, sure; I've got a little bit of experience. I'm sure I can learn whatever you give me." My answer must have been satisfactory, and he quickly waved me to follow him to the back shop, where the radio programmers and repair techs worked. "I know you must be bored to death with doing that paperwork stuff up there. I'm running behind on getting these radios programmed, and I'm going to show you how to do this one time. If you don't screw this up, we might be able to use you back here." He was a straight shooter. Short and to the point, but he had a sort of mentoring way about him. He broke out this metallic-wrapped cellophane bag and pulled an unusual-looking cord out of it. It had a jack on one side with a bunch of copper pins, and the other side had a serial port with two small thumb screws. "This is how we program radios. Watch what I do."

He quickly ran me through the process. Look at the sales order, pull the frequencies from the customer database, hook the cable up to the radio, make sure you touch the metal rack on the wall to discharge static so you don't blow a fuse in the cord, and a few other steps. He went pretty quickly and was firm with his direction. He didn't seem like the type of guy that would give me a second chance. I watched what he did intensely without saying a word. "Now you do one," he said.

I grabbed a new radio and repeated his steps exactly. Discharge the static, hook up the cable, download the old program, override it with the new frequencies, etc. Now that we had the first two radios programmed, he told me to always check my work to ensure both radios could transmit and receive. "Okay, good work. You seem like you could be a quick learner," he said gruffly with no inflection. "Get through this bin of radios, and we'll see what we can do with you." He shoved a massive bin of radios towards me and charged out of the room.

I went to work and banged through them as quickly as I could. I was ecstatic that I had even got an opportunity to learn a new skill, let alone only three weeks into the job. Is this what the working world was like? I could have been stuck pulling weeds or bagging groceries for twenty years. I was only at this place for three weeks and already learning new things! I was thrilled. Once I got through the bin of radios, I guess I'd passed the guy's test. Although my primary job was to be stuck in the back senselessly, logging data and filing papers, the opportunities kept coming. Since this was Manhattan, most of our deliveries were accomplished on foot. I started getting drop-off orders of batches of new or recently repaired radios to run all over the city. He also taught me how to run the Pitney Bowes postage machine back in the shipping area. When the programmers got backed up again, they would steal me to their offices so that I could help them get caught up on orders. I even got to learn some more advanced programming techniques like repeater systems as time went on. I'd been there for over a few months and was having a blast. I appreciated the opportunity to learn, and I started thinking more about what my place in this working world would be.

One day, a guy I didn't recognize came into the shop. I knew he was an employee because he had the same navy blue polo shirt we all wore, but I was surprised that I'd never seen him before. He walked right back into the programmer's office and started talking with my boss. They both came out only a short time later and charged back down the hall towards my workstation. "Hey, kid, grab your stuff; we're short on guys, and you're going to work in the field today." Unbeknownst to me, not only did the company sell and repair handheld radios, but they also wired and installed radio antenna systems for commercial buildings all over NYC. I had no idea they had an installation team, which explains why I'd never seen this guy.

Without hesitation, I followed the guy out and jumped into the elevator. He was much older than me and had a weathered look. He talked fast and walked fast. Even at seventeen, I had to practically jog to keep up with him as we turned the corner to pick up the work van. He didn't make much small talk other than asking my name and expressing his concerns about getting a parking ticket while running up to the shop. I jumped in the van, and we headed out. I had no idea what I was about to get into or where we were headed. I asked some direct questions, and he was quick to answer. He was happy to talk about work, job sites, and radios, but I could tell he wasn't much for personal small talk. He told me they had the contract on a new skyscraper going up in midtown Manhattan, and we had to finish getting some cabling in before the building got too far along. He had a serious energy about it.

He drove fast and impatiently tapped his non-brake foot on the floorboards whenever we got stuck at a red light. He seemed eager to get to the job site and genuinely excited about what he did for a living. He had a rough way about him, and his hands were huge, wrinkled, calloused, and battered. He looked like the kind of guy who had a lot of miles on him. I was a little intimidated by him, but at seventeen, my main concern was acting cool and laying low so that these guys had no reason to get tired of a young kid hanging around. After all, this could be the opportunity of a lifetime. I had no idea what we were about to get into.

We pulled up to the job site, and this guy flew out of the van like a bat out of hell. He already had the double doors of the van open by the time I unbuckled my seatbelt. "Come on, let's load up the tools," he hollered at me as I clumsily rushed to the back of the van. "We need this, two of these. Where's that other freakin' thing, dammit..." He muttered to himself as he piled things onto a push cart. I was amazed at how quickly he identified all the different parts. They all looked the same to me. "Come on, wheezy, let's go." (Almost two decades later, I don't know why he called me wheezy on good days and jackass on bad days, but that's a whole other story.)

We pulled the cart through the front doors of a new building under the scaffolding, and I felt like we entered a new world. It was a world I didn't know existed. I'd seen construction sites in movies and pictures, but this was the real deal. The atmosphere was electric! There were guys from every trade going every which way—tough guys with hard hats and forearm tattoos. The steelworkers were rigging up the I-beams. The ceiling installers were snapping grid into place. The framers were sawing metal studs, sparks flying out of the saw blades. There were masons and plumbers and electricians and drywallers. The place was crawling with people. It was loud as hell, and everyone was shouting at each other.

It was like a concert of skilled movements. Everyone was so precise and masterful of their craft. I felt frozen, but my new hyper speed manager marched us right to the work area and flung open a step ladder. He immediately started unreeling a roll of this thick, heavy black cable and instructed me to keep the reel moving as he sent it flying into the dropped ceiling. Before I knew it, he snapped around and jumped off the ladder. He cut the cable with a pair of pliers and stuffed the cut end back into the wooden reel in one quick, fluid motion. I was in shock at how fast this guy was moving. How did he know exactly where to go and what to do? How did he know exactly what trades to talk to and what questions to ask? I didn't even know if we were done with the job or not.

"Okay, let's hit the next stop. We're far enough along to where we can let the sheetrockers keep going." How did he even know that? I had so many questions. I had never had a sip of alcohol in my life, but I felt drunk on the atmosphere. We stacked the cart up and flew back out of there to the van, dodging guys with conduit and metal studs over their shoulders as they yelled orders and curse words to each other over the sounds of banging hammers and scraping metal. We got through the front entry and were ejected back into the bright midtown summer street. The noise faded instantly, like we'd gone through a portal. We threw the tools back into the van so fast I wasn't even sure we'd forgotten anything. I sprinted up to the cab and jumped in so we could hit the next job site.

My head was still spinning from the atmosphere. It was rough and tough, chaotic but fascinating. The energy was unmistakable. I was hooked. How the hell do these guys know how to just show up to work and build a skyscraper? Everyone did their part but in perfect synchrony. The most impressive thing I'd done up to that point was program a radio. I had to know more. I couldn't stop thinking about it for the rest of the day as we hit our next few stops. The whole train ride home, I was still intoxicated by the action. I had a strong feeling I had found what I wanted to do for the rest of my life. My next goal was to figure out how to keep those opportunities coming and pick the right trade to keep those doors open.

Those early experiences set the stage for the rest of my career. They ignited my drive and determination, and I just couldn't wait to see where the electrical trade would take me. After leaving the radio company, I got in as an apprentice doing residential and light commercial wiring. From there, I got into some heavier-duty commercial projects and had my first opportunity to run a job as a foreman. It was a forty thousand square foot build-out for a welding and machine shop. I'd finally obtained my journeyman electrician's license, and that project meant the world to me.

I served as an electrical and environmental maintenance technician in the United States Air Force, working on the

B-52 bomber. I worked as an electrician on some Army Corps of Engineers projects for Uncle Sam, a door opened to me through my military service. I passed my electrical contractors test and went out into my own business. I did that for seven years and had a lifetime of new experiences and challenges along the way (that's a whole story on its own). I currently serve as a project manager and electrical estimator for a commercial firm, and I can tell you from experience that the opportunities will keep coming. After fifteen years in the trade, I was lucky enough to be offered a position as a part-time instructor at a technical college, which opened an entirely new set of doors. I also help develop curriculum for an online electrical training platform.

I hope you can use this book to help you navigate your way through your apprenticeship. You'll have stories from this career field that your friends and family won't believe. An electrical apprenticeship is as far as you'll get from a desk job. While office workers tell you stories of watching the clock all day and praying for the monotony to end, you'll have stories of troubleshooting complex motor control systems, climbing on the tops of buildings, and crawling through high-voltage underground vaults. I've worked on massive jet engines troubleshooting generator issues. I've worked in trenches assembling banks of galvanized steel conduit that required brute force and in high-end restaurants assembling chandeliers that required the most careful finesse. There are challenges and unique experiences around every corner of the electrical world. But before you find any success in this trade, you have to remember that you can't be afraid to work!

Chapter 1

Why Choose Electrical Over College? Making The Case For The Trades

As technology advances, it seems fewer and fewer people are interested in hands-on work. The COVID-19 pandemic has ushered in a new norm of "work from home" opportunities where remote work has replaced much of the work previously done in offices. Career opportunities exist that were unheard of not very long ago. Social media manager? Blogger? These jobs simply didn't exist before. There are now opportunities to roll out of bed in your pajamas, log onto a laptop, and start clocking hours for a paycheck. This phenomenon has only been further exacerbated by the social media boom.

Now, I'm not knocking anyone who works remotely (my wife happens to be one of them). I'm simply probing the question, "Why get into a skilled trade?" Office work is more comfortable. You're in the air conditioning in the summer and the heat in the winter. You may have the comforts of home while you work or work in a fancy office with snacks, drinks, and unlimited amenities. Skilled trade work can be grueling at times. There are some hard days. You'll get dirty. You'll sweat in the summer working on a roof. You'll freeze in the winter, getting whipped by the wind outside. You'll get blisters and cuts on your hands. So why would *anyone* in their right mind choose to make a living like that over a comfortable, climate-controlled office?

Variety

There are many people out there, and I am definitely included in this camp, who get bored easily. Part of what draws people to the trades, especially electrical, is the constant variety of work. You might be on a large construction project for months on end, or you might be doing four service calls a day. You might wire a boat dock at a marina or be underground in a vault, splicing cable. You can go from ethernet cabling to lighting to transformers in a single week. The nature of the work is varied, and if you work for a company that performs multiple facets of electrical work, you're much more likely to run into these variations.

What's really interesting about the constant variety is the fast pace and the learning opportunities. If you've heard the term "one trick pony," then imagine being a well-rounded electrician is the polar opposite of that. Those of us who get bored have the comfort of knowing that our next challenge is right around the corner. Not only will the variety of work be different, but the locations will change constantly, too. Unless you're a maintenance electrician permanently assigned to one location, there is a 100 percent chance you will go where the work is. You'll work in different cities, maybe even in different states. I've worked on everything from downtown high-rise office buildings to farms out in the

CHAPTER 1

sticks and just about everything in between. It's hard to get bored when you go to more places in a week than most people are used to going to in a month.

Pride Of Working With Your Hands

There is just something about the pride of working with your hands that's hard to explain. Sure, many people tinker around with cars, motorcycles, or houses in their spare time, but doing it for a living starts to become deeply meaningful. It's as though our nature pushes us to be physically connected to something rather than just mentally connected. Think about it. Why do sports exist? If we didn't have some desire to pursue physical activities, football would never have been created, and everyone would just play chess. Some of us are more drawn to physical work than others. And it is those types of people that might find a lot of satisfaction in a skilled trade.

There is almost an endorphin rush after putting in an honest day's work and giving it everything you've got. It's sort of like getting a good workout in. Your blood is pumping, your hands are dirty and calloused, and you're exhausted for all the right reasons. You get to look back with pride on what YOU accomplished with YOUR own two hands. There's a great feeling of satisfaction. You've just solved a problem for someone or made much-needed improvements to a building. Adding value to the world can be a fantastic experience you can relive daily in a different capacity. Maybe an electrical issue brought down an entire office and forced a business to grind to a halt. Your mechanical skills and knowledge of troubleshooting saved the day and helped the business world keep turning so that other people could make a living. Remember, without light and power, our modern world stops dead in its tracks.

Active Work

Working with your hands gives you more than just variety and satisfaction; it promotes a truly active lifestyle. It's hard work! Some people like to poke fun at the electricians, saying it's a "clean trade." The people who say this are people who a) have never done electrical work or b) have never actually made a living working with their hands. Install some 4" rigid metallic conduit, pull 500 kcmil copper conductors through it, and tell me that electrical is clean or easy. I would challenge anyone to do so.

The fact is that electrical work is active, busy work, and it can be physically challenging. There is very little downtime. You might spend all day snaking wires through a scorching hot attic, swinging around a 32-foot fiberglass extension ladder, or bending 1-¼" metal conduit. The fun part is that you can almost treat it like a sport. There may be beautiful summer days when you're working on the beach. You get fresh air and move your body, all while keeping your mind engaged and active.

Endless Opportunity

There are also arguably more money-making opportunities today than at any other time in human history. Could your great-grandfather have imagined social media managers, cryptocurrency traders, or TikTok influencers? Despite our changing world, for the last one or two generations, many high school students have been blindly pushed into college—even clueless high school seniors are told just to pick a college and figure out a major later. The skilled trades have long been looked at as a backup plan for the kids who aren't "college material." I certainly hope that this book can help to break that stereotype.

CHAPTER 1

Don't get me wrong; I don't want to glamorize the trades any more than I want to discredit white-collar pursuits. There is no right or wrong path, and the one you choose depends on your personality and particular career goals. However, I hope I can do justice to highlighting some of the benefits of pursuing a career in the electrical trade.

- ⚡ Job growth. The average age of a licensed electrician ticks up year after year. As electricians get older and retire, enrollments in trade programs are simply not keeping pace. What that means for you is that there are not enough young people in the trades to replace the people retiring. This labor gap presents a unique opportunity for you if you're willing to capture it

- ⚡ Niche Opportunities. The opportunities within the electrical trade are so vast that it's almost overwhelming. The electrical trade is growing rapidly, and electricity is becoming increasingly crucial to keep our society running and our world turning. The advent of electric vehicles, solar energy, smart lighting controls, and the IoT (internet of things), to name a few, have produced extreme demand and made us ever more dependent on electricity. This new technology has created niche opportunities within the electrical trade that didn't even exist for the previous generation. Not all electricians are simply residential, commercial, or industrial electricians. You might specialize in battery storage systems. Maybe you'll focus on mastering photovoltaic (solar) work. You may decide that you enjoy fire alarm cabling and system programming while your friend wants to go after smart lighting controls. The industry is growing every day, and it's growing faster than ever. The opportunity to specialize and carve a niche for yourself may present some unique opportunities.

⚡ Management opportunities. Not all electricians stay on their tools for their entire careers. The specialized electrical knowledge you'll accumulate while working in the field may open doors you never knew existed. Some of these positions might include but not be limited to:

- ⚡ Service manager: Someone has to schedule the guys and put the puzzle pieces together to keep the work orders flowing

- ⚡ Project Manager: Are you an effective communicator who likes to solve problems? You'll help keep the project on scope and within budget, figuring out the tools and resources the guys in the field will need to keep pace with the project schedule. You'll meet with general contractors, plumbers, carpenters, excavators, and engineers to figure out how to support each person's part of the project moving along as it should

- ⚡ Superintendent or Foreman: You might discover that you're a natural-born leader. Someone has to be the face of the crew and lead the team to victory. This position takes someone with good judgment and can handle making many decisions quickly. You might need to do some mentoring and teaching along the way to make sure your team can work as a cohesive unit

- ⚡ Estimator: Do you like being behind the scenes? The estimator is the first person to wrap their head around the plans for a new building. You'll have to figure out how long the work will take and what materials will be needed. You might have to negotiate with vendors and subcontractors and write up proposals. You'll be the first step

CHAPTER 1

in making sure the company stays profitable. Estimating a large, complicated project may require you to be part engineer/part lawyer while still flexing your electrical skills as you navigate technical data and convoluted contract terms

The opportunities don't stop there. The sky's the limit as long as you continue to look for opportunities. If you're really ambitious, you may decide to get your contractor's license and start a business of your own.

Electrical work can be satisfying on many levels. You might be troubleshooting an extremely complicated problem. When you finally solve it and have that "a-ha!" moment, you'll feel the rush that comes with being the hero of the day. On the other hand, you might spend the next day running large conduit in the bottom of a trench or pulling heavy copper conductors off a massive wooden reel. You'll be working hard, oftentimes out in the elements, moving your body and keeping the blood flowing. Nothing feels better than the satisfaction of a hard day's work! It's something you can be proud of at the end of a long day.

Could There Be More To It? A Note On The Feel-good Brain Response From Working With Your Hands:

Of course the electrical trade is one of the few lucrative careers that you can still enter without the need to take on student debt, not every career decision is purely financial. There is another aspect to choosing a career and it boils down to one simple word: happiness. What are you going to be happy doing for 40 hours a week for the next 40 years of your life?

Take teaching as an example. Money is probably one of the least regarded aspects when considering a career in the teaching profession. Surely you can make more money being a stockbroker than a teacher. So why choose teaching? It just goes to show you that there are many different factors that come into play when choosing a career. You'll make more money as a stockbroker than a teacher, but what about the mission? Some people have a deep pull to teaching because they believe in the greater purpose. They see how important it is to teach the next generation and to give something back. They see how they can make a difference in their community and how crucial a role the development of kids and young adults can be in the long run. There are other people who don't have thoughts like this and they just want to make as much money as humanly possible. That is fine too and there is certainly nothing wrong with that, but blindly chasing money is not for everyone. Sometimes it comes down to quality over quantity.

This mentality is often applied to the skilled trades as well. There is no doubt that electrical work, plumbing, welding, and carpentry are more physically demanding than banking, accounting, or selling insurance. But some of us are perfectly fine with that. In fact, many of us actually prefer it. We find the work fun and challenging. We see ourselves as craftsmen or artisans that produce an amazing product which takes years of diligent practice to master. We have active personalities and don't like being cooped up inside. These are all personality traits, but there might actually be something to it that's much deeper: something that drives us to seek this type of work on a psychological level. It is a theory called the *effort driven rewards cycle* that was popularized a few years back by neuroscientist Kelly Lambert. It basically boils down to this: working with your hands feels good. Doing physical work where you can touch, feel,

CHAPTER 1

and see the results of your efforts fires up parts of the brain that release feel-good chemicals. It's the reward for your hard-earned efforts. This could likely be an evolutionary tool that we've developed in order to survive. Your brain is rewarded when you physically exert yourself. Thousands of years ago, if you did not move and work hard, you would die. The ancient ancestor who spent hours chasing a wild boar or searching for edible plants survived and passed on their genes. The ancestor that stayed inactive, lethargic, or sedentary simply starved or was killed by a predator. Now I am by no means any kind of scientist but I can tell you anecdotally over my two decades of doing electrical work that I couldn't agree with this more. There is a sort of instant gratification that comes from doing work with your hands.

If you've ever done any gardening, cooking, or working on cars you probably know what I'm talking about. Getting your hands dirty just feels good for reasons we can't quite put into words. There is a certain pride and satisfaction that swells up when you physically work hard on something. With skilled trades work, you get to experience this satisfaction in a variety of ways day after day. It may lead to more job satisfaction and as well as overall satisfaction about your life. Of course not everyday will feel like this. Matter of fact there will be many days where you feel flat out deflated and defeated. You'll screw something up that sets a job back. You'll wire something wrong and blow up a piece of equipment. You'll struggle endlessly with small parts that just don't seem to go together. But you'll find in the long run that you'll have many more wins than losses; many more victories than defeats. It takes persistence which further feeds into that feel-good response. You'll be rewarded in the short term by those proud feelings of making or fixing something with your own hands, but in the long term as well by committing to the journey of mastering a craft that many people simply aren't capable of doing. It's a double benefit and while we may not make as much as stockbrokers or lawyers, I wouldn't trade it for anything.

Action Items

✓ Research jobs in your area. Are any apprenticeship opportunities currently available? Send out five resumes and follow up with a phone call.

✓ Revamp your resume. If you don't have much work experience, highlight your other attributes like your reliability or work ethic. Have a friend or colleague review it and give you feedback.

✓ Find out how much money licensed electricians make in your area.

✓ Make a list of likes and dislikes regarding your work environment. Does electrical work suit your personality?

✓ Reach out to three local electrical contractors. Tell them you're interested in the career field and ask if you can job shadow for a day.

Chapter 2

The Misconceptions Of The "Back Up Plan"

One thing that disappoints me about how the general public views the construction trades is that it's looked at as a backup career. It's as if no one plans to enter a career in the trades; they simply "end up" there. Here are actual conversations I've had with people over the years:

- ⚡ "I'm going to try college, but if it doesn't work out, I guess I can always learn a trade."
- ⚡ "My kid isn't exactly college material. Do you think an electrical company would be willing to hire him?"
- ⚡ "My kid is a lazy bum who lives in my basement. I need to get him out of the house. Can you set him up with an electrical company so he can do something with his life?"
- ⚡ "My cousin just got out of prison. Can you set him up with a job so he can get his life back on track? Real companies won't hire him."

While I'm all for people getting their lives on track, why are the skilled trades the dumping ground for those lost in life? Why does electrical or plumbing or carpentry have to be something that you just "end up in" rather than a career path to strive for? As a society, we need to bring honor and dignity back to the skilled trades. We do important, meaningful work every day. We keep the economy going. We install and repair the systems that provide the very infrastructure the business world runs on. Next time you're able to get your question answered by Google in two nanoseconds, thank the electricians who built the data center. We need to promote the skilled trades in this country as a viable path for the best and brightest, not just the backup plan for when things don't work out.

Maybe that very logical student being pushed towards a career in software engineering would make an amazing troubleshooter on electrical systems. How about the kid with the amazing work ethic who the parents want to apply to medical school? He might absolutely dominate as an electrical contractor. We have a shortage of skilled labor in this country, and throwing bodies at the problem is not enough. We need to promote interest in these career fields to promising young people so we can continue to realize great achievements in this industry. Instead of asking if you should "try electrical if college doesn't work out," ask yourself, "Do I have what it takes to become a master electrician?"

There is a lot of prestige in becoming a master tradesman, whether it be electrical, plumbing, carpentry, or any other trade. While there are definitely other people out there now who are promoting the trades as a viable career path and bringing dignity, legitimacy, and respect back to this industry, it's a slow-moving ship, and it will take time and effort on all our parts. If you've tried to get any work done on your house lately, you'll understand how stark the skilled trade

CHAPTER 2

shortage has become. Tradesmen can be booked weeks out for small projects and months out for large ones. With an aging infrastructure and a reduced supply of skilled labor, you've got the perfect storm for a healthy resurgence of the skilled trades. The money is there, and there is no doubt that you can make a fine living.

I can attest to that, along with many other electricians and plumbers I'm friendly with, but you have to remember that it's no different than any other career in the sense that what you put in is what you get back. You won't have a smooth ride to the top simply because electricians are in demand. You must work at it, learn constantly, make smart career moves, network, and push yourself. Your end result will be determined by your level of dedication over the years.

The world of skilled tradespeople is full of amazing men and women. Everyone likes to stereotype the trades and think of the "plumber's crack" joke, but don't get caught up in these foolish and disparaging lies. Building and maintaining this country is important work. It is dignified. Without electricians, our modern world grinds to a halt. Imagine a business getting through the day without power, light, and the internet. It's simply impossible because we've built our entire society around it, and electricians are the people who play a vital role in keeping it turning. So, if you want to be a part of this amazing trade, or if you already are, remember to represent it well. Be a good example for the next generation of electricians and surround yourself with others who hold their heads high with pride and dignity. That's the only way we'll change the public perception of what the skilled trades truly are. If we're going to change anything, we need to do better. We must bring respect to all skilled trades and set good examples for current and future generations.

Public perception aside, another huge factor is at play here: the lack of getting into student debt as you pursue your career in the trade. Large student loans can be crippling for young people just getting their careers off the ground, especially for people who don't understand the basic economic concept of supply and demand when choosing their career field. It's very difficult to make huge life decisions at sixteen, seventeen, or eighteen years of age that will determine the course of your early career. In fact, it's arguably tougher than ever. Many kids out there simply aren't being presented with the correct information by their families and schools. They may be blindly pushed into college with little thought on what they will do and end up declaring a major they don't realize has very little demand or real-world application. Or they may pursue a field with an oversaturated labor pool and cut-throat competition, making it extremely difficult to compete in the marketplace with the glut of other qualified candidates.

There is a huge difference between someone who has undergone rigorous studies in law or medical school and someone who haphazardly picked a program with no end goal. The law or medical student may have put themselves on a direct path to an in-demand career, while the latter may have taken on unnecessary debt with the hopes that they eventually find a job they may be qualified to do. Let's look at a practical example of two friends. We'll call them Kelly and Mary.

Mary's parents have always pushed her towards college. The career counselors have supported this simply by not making her aware of any alternate path. Anything other than leaving high school and immediately going into college was never presented as a viable option by any parent, teacher, or faculty member. Neither of her parents were college-educated, and they've simply assumed that going to college is just "what you do" now. Mary has had a few fleeting career interests come and go over her high school years but has never really latched onto anything she found worth dedicating her energy to. She blindly follows the advice of her parents and the administration and enrolls in a college that two of her friends are interested in without doing much research.

On the other hand, Kelly's dad is a plumbing contractor who runs a small contracting business doing one-man jobs. Because of this, she's always been around the trades in one way or another. She's heard her dad's stories and even used to ride along and help him during a few summer breaks over the years. Her dad has never pushed Kelly one way or the other to commit to a career path, but he has kept a positive spotlight shining on the skilled trades as a possibility.

During her junior and senior years, they've talked many times about college, but he's been strict about ensuring that she has a plan. How will you fund your college education? Will you take on debt? Have you applied for scholarships and grants? Have you made a list of majors and checked them against the demand projections released annually by the Bureau of Labor Statistics? He even emailed and printed her a copy of the *Occupational Outlook Handbook* that the BLS releases every year so she can check various majors and career paths against what is *in demand* in the working world. Although he promotes college as a viable career path when pursued responsibly, he doesn't discount a career in the skilled trades. He's made a fine living for himself and is a good role model for someone who has leveraged market demand very well by matching his skill set to the economic opportunities of the day. He encourages Kelly to talk to an electrician friend of his, tour a local community college, and tour both a state and private university.

While Kelly sets out to do some serious research, Mary applies to one and only one college, which is the university that all of her friends attend. It's a decent school, and she's kept her grades high throughout high school, so she's not too worried about getting in. She sends her application in and then forgets about it while she spends the rest of high school enjoying time with her friends. Later that year, she receives an acceptance letter from the school. She's relieved but not very surprised. She knows quite a few people going to this college, including two close friends, and hasn't heard of anyone being rejected.

She unveils the acceptance letter that night at dinner with her parents, and they begin to discuss the plan. The in-state tuition costs are $12,000 per year. It doesn't seem like that much money, and her parents don't seem too worried about her taking on some debt. They figure she'll pay it back in no time once she gets into the workforce. Since neither of her parents are college graduates, they know nothing about the student loan process. "Does that include room and board?" her mom asks. "No, that's just the tuition," Mary replies.

This is their first time discussing the logistics of her future education, and her parents are both a little shocked to hear this. Twelve thousand dollars per year doesn't sound like much, but what are the other costs? They assume she'll be making a six-figure salary in no time upon graduation anyway, so they don't think much about it. Since the college is two hours away from their house, she'll need to pay for room and board. She'll also need to purchase a new laptop and pay for other books, supplies, and various fees.

They spend hours that night compiling all of the costs, and her parents are shocked at what they come up with. This $12,000 a year college is actually going to cost Mary $28,000 a year when they roll all of these other costs in. Her dad is getting a little nervous now, but Mary and her mom reassure him that all her friends are doing it, so there must be a way to make it work. They quickly Google some student loan options and find some federal loans available with 4 percent interest rates. That seems reasonable; it's less than the interest rate on their mortgage, and they've managed to swing that all these years. They forget about it and move on, and Mary spends the next few weeks securing financing with student loans. The repayment is deferred until she graduates, so she has four years before she has to worry about it again.

Meanwhile, Kelly researches her four options. Follow my dad into the trades? Start for cheap at a local community college and then transfer to a university? Spend four years at a state university? Or go all out on a private university and live the college life to the max? She crunches all the numbers, and much like Mary's parents, she's a little shocked about the true cost of college. She knows her dad has set some money aside over the years for her, but it doesn't even scratch the surface. The four-year private university option would come out to $189,000 once she factored in room and board, books, supplies, and fees on top of the base tuition cost. Her dad has always talked to her about compound interest and the importance of saving for retirement early, so she understands how interest plays into the equation. At 4 percent, she is not comfortable with the financial projections, so she rules out the four-year private university as a realistic option.

She still considers the in-state and community colleges, but after a really interesting conversation with her dad's electrician friend, her mind is made up! She doesn't see the negative stereotypes about the construction trades often portrayed in the media and other professional circles. Her dad is a perfect gentleman and has always been highly regarded by his family and local community. She feels the same about the electrician and trusts his advice. However, she is reluctant about being a female in a male-dominated industry. While it is true that over 96 percent of electricians are men, her dad and his friend encourage her not to be intimidated by this. She is a mature, hard-working kid and has become a confident young woman. They assure her that her work ethic and basic mechanical skills will earn her the same respect as the boys once she gets in there and proves herself.

The next four years fly by. Mary is busy having fun at college. Her parents encourage her not to think about the student debt. This is her time to be young and free, not to worry about money. As long as she's keeping her grades up, they're happy. She'll find a job as soon as she graduates.

Kelly is busy working hard at learning the electrical trade and proving herself to the guys at work. The first six months are pretty rough, but as her skills and knowledge progress, her coworkers start to see her potential. Her dad encourages her to work hard and treat her new career seriously but also reminds her to have fun with her friends on weekends and work nights when she doesn't have her apprenticeship classes.

Shortly after her eighteenth birthday, Kelly's dad starts talking to her about saving for retirement. "Retirement? I'm less than a year into my career. Why worry about retirement now?" Kelly objects. Her dad laughs because this is exactly the reaction he was expecting. They sit down with her company's 401k enrollment application and review the nuts and bolts of retirement plans. First, her dad explains that retirement accounts like 401ks and IRAs are *tax-advantaged* accounts, meaning that contributions to the plan lower your taxable income since you won't pay taxes on the money until you retire and start to draw down the account.

For example, if you make $65,000 this year and you contribute $8,000 of that to a pre-tax retirement account like a 401k, you'll only be taxed on $57,000 worth of income. Kelly is not exactly blown away by this; she still finds financial talk pretty boring. "Okay, this isn't the most exciting thing in the world, but I bet compound interest will blow your mind," Kelly's dad challenges. He tells Kelly she'll need about a million dollars saved in her account by the time she retires. Kelly is completely shocked at hearing that. "One million dollars? How can I possibly save that amount of money? That's just not realistic". But her dad patiently explains that through compound interest, it's not only possible, but it's easily achievable with the right game plan.

The beauty of compound interest is that it begins to multiply your savings. If you deposit $100 in an account that yields a 5 percent interest rate, you'll have $105. If that interest rate never changes, you would think you would go from $105 to $110 to $115 and so forth, slowly accumulating interest, but that is not true due to the magic of compound interest. You would actually gain interest on your principal balance, which is now $105. Five percent interest on that now brings your balance up to $110.25. You've gained an extra 25 cents just for letting your money accumulate in an account.

It doesn't sound like much, but over your career, this is extremely powerful. Kelly's dad grabs his laptop and brings up a compound interest calculator. (There are tons of them out there, but I like the simple layout of www.investor.gov). He tells Kelly that they will start with $100 a week. It doesn't sound like much, but let's see how much it adds up to by the time Kelly is set to retire. If Kelly is eighteen now and wants to retire at sixty-five, she has forty-seven years to work, save, and let compound interest work its magic. Her dad plugs a simple formula into the compound interest calculator:

Starting Balance: $0 (this will be her first time saving)

Monthly Contribution: $400 (Kelly will commit to saving $100 per week)

Length of Time: 47 years (Kelly will start to draw down the account at 65)

Estimated Interest Rate: 7% (this is what the stock market has historically returned over time through the ups and downs of the market)

Result: $1,580,277.05

Kelly is blown away by this. She can't believe that a minor amount of savings could make her a millionaire one day. She and her dad start plugging in all kinds of numbers for fun. If she were saving $100 a week without investing it, she would have only ended up with $225,600 at the end. That means she would have missed out on $1,354,677 worth of compound interest! She wonders if she would be able to save more aggressively once she starts making more money. She plugs in $200 a week to see what that would yield. That brings her ending balance up to $3,160,554.11 after forty-seven years. Kelly is astonished by the law of compound interest and all its possibilities. She is sold. That night, her dad helps her complete the enrollment form, and they scan it over to her boss. Two weeks after her eighteenth birthday, Kelly is on the road to becoming a millionaire.

Mary, meanwhile, has yet to have an opportunity to begin saving. She's four years into college, and graduation is nearly in sight. During her last semester, she meets with the school's finance office to review her loan obligations once she graduates. She sits at the desk, and the school's finance administrator spins a computer monitor around to review the numbers. She sees that her tuition, room and board, and other costs turned out to be $28,780 per year. It's a little higher than she expected to pay, but she didn't consider that

CHAPTER 2

the school would gradually raise tuition rates throughout her time there. Her principal balance is $115,120. She's not too surprised to see that because, in her head, she always knew that she'd be facing a six-figure bill. She figures she'll pay it off in no time once she gets an amazing job that pays a ton of money.

The administrator then adds the interest. Mary remembers her dad saying something about 4 percent back when she started, and luckily, that interest rate was locked in. That doesn't sound like much, so Mary isn't worried about it. The administrator plugs in 4 percent for interest and twenty years for the repayment period. "Twenty years!" Mary challenges. "I can't be in debt for twenty years." The administrator unsympathetically explains that Mary will never be able to make the payment if she goes for less than a twenty-year term. At a 4 percent interest rate over twenty years, the monthly payment will be $697.60. If she drops the loan repayment term down to ten years, the monthly payment climbs to $1,165.53.

Mary is shocked to see this. Her stomach drops into her shoes. How can this be? How did my parents not warn me about this? She thought she would pay her loans off in about five years, but she never considered it seriously enough to run her numbers. Just out of curiosity, she asks the administrator to plug in a five-year loan term. The administrator shrugs her off and tells her that no one will ever use a five-year term unless they are getting help from their parents, but she plugs it in just to humor Mary. The monthly payment is $2,120.11! That's more than her parents pay a month for their mortgage. She reluctantly agrees to the twenty-year term and leaves the office disheartened and overwhelmed.

She manages to forget about it for a little while as she prepares to graduate. She's done very well in school and graduates in the top 10 percent of her class. She takes the summer off to spend time with her family. She remembers the administrator telling her that the student loans have a six-month deferment period from graduation. She's a college graduate. She's got it made. Companies will come knocking on her door, begging her to join their ranks.

September rolls around, and that six-month deferment period seems to be slipping away by the day. Mary decides it's time to pound the pavement and nail that dream job. She starts looking around online for jobs but is disappointed to see that there isn't much out there specific to her major. The postings that do mention it often require a master's degree or ten years of work experience. The thought of going into more debt is out of the question. And ten years of experience? How is she supposed to get that if her bachelor's degree won't get her in the door?

About eight months after graduation, Mary finally accepts an offer from a company. It's not exactly what she wanted to do, and the money isn't great, but at this point, she realizes that she just needs to get her foot in the door and move on with her life. She'll move up through the ranks eventually. At least it's a start. The job pays $26 an hour. After taxes and the company's healthcare deduction, she brings home $780 a week. She's feeling pretty good until she remembers her student loan payment.

Monthly Net Income: $3,120

Student Loan Payment: $697

Money Left To Live On: $2,423

Mary is feeling pretty bleak about her career situation. What about a new car? She's still driving her uncle's old hand-me-down beater. A working professional needs a nice car. Unfortunately, she has no credit, so she'll pay the highest possible interest rate. The monthly payment on the car she wants

CHAPTER 2

is $540 a month, bringing her remaining income to $1,853. She starts looking for apartments nearby, but most rents are between $1,600 and $1,750 a month. This doesn't leave enough for food, insurance, gas, and other living expenses. Should she hold out on the car? Should she live at home for a few more years? Should she refinance her student loan into a thirty-year term? Should she look for a roommate?

Mary is very disappointed at how this is all shaking out. She decides to go for the new car because the old beater is starting to give her trouble. The car is $38,000, but her dad borrows from his 401k to help her with the down payment. She has yet to start a 401k of her own. She has $3,000 in an emergency savings account that she scraped together with odd jobs. Her net worth is (-$148,120).

Meanwhile, Kelly is nearing the end of the first four years of her career and begins to prepare to take her journeyman electrician's exam. The last four years have been a whirlwind. She's learned a lot, but not without many mistakes, recoveries, trials, and tribulations. As she rose through the ranks and proved herself more and more, the raises came along with her level of effort and mastery of electrical work. After the first year, she bought a used car on a three-year loan. It was a little tight initially because she was also contributing to her 401k, but after receiving another raise six months later, she could afford it more comfortably. By the time she was ready to sit for her test, the car was paid off, and she was sitting on a good start towards her retirement. Any night or weekend overtime she worked went into savings for a new car, vacation, tools, or other expenses. By year three, she was able to afford her own place.

Six months out from taking her journeyman exam, Kelly hits the books hard. She is determined to pass the test on her first attempt. She hears stories around work of people taking two or three tries to pass it, but this is not an option for her. Her dad passed both his journeyman and master plumbing exams on the first try, and he knows with absolute certainty his daughter is capable of doing the same. She does twenty-five practice exam questions every night after work. On Saturdays, she carves out at least four hours for deep study on electrical theory, motor controls, transformers, load calculations, and more.

Although she's been going to night school for the past four years to fulfill the educational requirements for the apprenticeship program, it's this last six months that she gets to know the codebook front to back through diligent self-study. The exam day comes, and she cruises through it without breaking a sweat. The next Monday, her boss congratulates her and hands her an envelope with a document outlining the payscale she's being promoted to. He encourages her to keep learning and to push for her master electrician's license in a few years when she's ready. For now, she'll be the lead electrician on a large project with plans to become a foreman on the next small job they start. If she manages that well, she'll get a 15 percent raise and be awarded the title of foreman, responsible for running larger projects and working directly with the project managers. Her strategic career moves are paying off, and the future looks bright.

Monthly Net Income: $3,970

Car Value (Paid Off): $11,800

Savings Account Balance: $13,500

Retirement Account Balance: $9,300

Net Worth: $34,600

Credit Score: 690

Age: 22

Bachelor's Degree: None

CHAPTER 2

To Recap

What you get out of it = what you put into it. We all hear these stories about people who get lucky and strike it rich, but I think there are fewer people like that than we like to believe. Kelly was focused and diligent. She had a plan and a good role model. She weighed her options, did her research, and considered the advice of those around her. There were times during her apprenticeship when she wanted to quit. The trades can be an extremely challenging work environment, but she persisted. She saved her money and put her long-term wealth over her short-term wants.

There will be people who get through their apprenticeship faltering, failing to learn from mistakes, and making poor financial decisions. There will be people who get through their apprenticeships and go on to become successful foremen, estimators, project managers, and business owners. The same can be said for those who take the traditional college path. Your end results will ultimately be defined by your attitude and willingness to work on making your chosen path work for YOU.

After a four-year apprenticeship, you can be a competent and successful individual. You can hold your head high and gain the respect of those in your family and your community. You can create opportunities for others by starting a business, or you can help further the trade by teaching young apprentices. The people living these ideals are NOT the parodied high school dropouts of yesteryear. This industry is full of amazing people with the skills and knowledge needed to provide a good life for themselves and their families. Next time someone discourages you from not going to college, challenge them to see it another way and not be blind to other opportunities.

Action Items

✓ Talk with family, friends, and neighbors. Are any of them electricians or tradesmen in a related field? Offer to buy lunch for someone in exchange for picking their brain for information and guidance.

✓ Schedule an appointment to tour a local technical program, community college, or trade school.

✓ If you're already working, open an Individual Retirement Account (IRA). When you land an apprenticeship with a company that offers a 401k, you can always roll over what you've saved on your own into the company plan.

✓ Save 5 percent of your income and see how it goes for three months. Can you get your savings up to 10 percent and still make ends meet?

✓ Visit investor.gov and play around with the compound interest calculator. You'll be amazed at how much of a difference saving money can make when you start young.

Chapter 3

Landing Your First Job As An Apprentice

Now, this may seem counterintuitive, knowing that the field is in such high demand, but landing your first apprenticeship can be extremely difficult for a variety of reasons. Even though there is a major shortage of electricians, we need *qualified electricians*. So what you have is a long-term process here. If a seventeen-year-old high school grad is interested in the electrical trade, that's great news! Unfortunately, he won't be of much use to an electrical contractor for two to four years just based on the nature of how much there is to learn to become proficient. He'll likely start as a gopher (fetching parts from the van, unloading deliveries on a job site) and then graduate to a helper (working more closely with the licensed electricians and senior apprentices).

To further complicate matters, your state may have hiring ratios that limit the amount of unlicensed personnel a company can employ at any given time. I can't speak to other states, but I can tell you how it works in my home state of Connecticut. In Connecticut, there is a hiring ratio that limits the number of unlicensed to licensed employees in a company and on a job site. For example, if we have two licensed electricians employed at a small company, we can also have two apprentices. If one of those apprentices can fulfill his school and work requirements (720 school hours and eight thousand work hours here), he is eligible to sit for his journeyman electrician licensing exam. If he passes the test and gets his license, the company now has three licensed electricians and one apprentice.

This move has now opened up a slot for two new apprentices. We now have three license holders and up to three apprentices until the next guy passes his test. It sounds like a great path of growth for the company in theory, but where the rubber meets the road, it falls short. What if this apprentice fails his exam? What if he leaves the company? He can be replaced with a new apprentice, but let's say he was 7,500 (out of eight thousand) hours into the apprenticeship when he left, and his replacement is starting the apprenticeship program from scratch. You were only months away from the opportunity to grow your business as the owner, but now, this new employee will take four years to become licensed. I hope you didn't just sign that big contract in hopes that you were about to hire more manpower!

The other catch-22 this creates is the disconnect in the narrative between opportunities in the trade and available apprenticeships. For example, there is a lot of talk these days about how the trades are once again getting the respect they deserve as a viable career path. Everyone is aware that our dependence on electricity has laid fertile ground for us to thrive for many years as an industry. A young potential apprentice may hear this and think, "There are so many opportunities in this industry; I'll find a job in no time."

CHAPTER 3

Unfortunately, how this plays out is often a sad state of affairs. Let's say a seventeen-year-old high school graduate makes the decision to become an electrician. He goes to a company that employs two licensed journeyman electricians and two apprentices and applies for a job. One apprentice is six months into his four-year apprenticeship, and the other is one year in. This means, at the very minimum, if the existing apprentice does everything perfectly, learns what he needs to learn, takes no time off, and passes his exam on the first try, the earliest possible time frame the high school grad could gain employment with this company is three years. And that's if the stars align! By then, he'll be twenty years old, and his college-bound peers will already be thinking about wrapping up their bachelor's degrees. I would expect very few people to wait three years for a job opportunity.

So here we've sent the message that the electrical trade is blowing up. Blue-collar workers are going to be the next millionaires. The baby boomers are retiring in droves and need to be replaced with new skilled workers. But in the same breath, we've denied an opportunity to someone who is truly eager, and we've dammed that entire flow of potential progress. The seventeen-year-old grad is now forced to simply apply to more and more companies in the hopes that one of them is "within ratio." Hopefully, he lives in an area with ample electrical contractors, so he is not forced to commute for hours to an opportunity. As you can imagine, this rejection can hurt the trade by sending mixed messages.

On the other side of the same coin, the ratios were implemented originally for good reason. You wouldn't want a crew of twenty first-year apprentices with only one or two qualified individuals building a large project. You need a mix of varying skill levels where the very knowledgeable seasoned vets run the project, the journeymen perform the intricate work, and the apprentices soak up the learning opportunities while performing the grunt work.

This being said, don't get discouraged if you're genuinely interested in pursuing a career in the electrical trade. Here are some tips that might help to get you in the door faster to get your career up and running:

- ⚡ If you can't find an electrical job immediately, get on a waiting list while working a general construction job. It will build up your work ethic, and you'll learn your way around a job site while you wait for a slot to open up.

- ⚡ Use another trade as a stepping stone. Let's say you've picked the company that you've got your sights set on. They seem like such a great company to work for, and that's where you need to be. If they have a year-long waiting list, maybe you can gain a year of experience in an adjacent trade for your skills to transfer over. Maybe an HVAC, fire alarm, or network cabling firm has an opportunity for you while you set your sights on your long-term goals.

- ⚡ Be open to options. Would you be willing to relocate if needed? Would you consider working for an industrial firm when you originally had your sights set on residential?

- ⚡ Network at the supply houses. The supply houses are often like the bars and barbershops of the tradesman's world. There is a lot of talk between companies and between vendors. You may discover that the oldest apprentice at XYZ Electric is only two months away from his journeyman exam, so his slot is very close to opening up. You have to strike fast and get in there now to secure your future.

CHAPTER 3

- Pursue both union and non-union or "open shop" apprenticeship programs. I won't get into detail on "union vs. non-union." They are both excellent avenues, but the right choice for you can depend on a variety of factors. I would encourage you to research organizations like the IBEW and the IEC for more information to make an informed decision. I would also highly recommend talking to individuals on both sides of the industry.

If you want something badly enough and you're smart, strategic, and willing to work hard, you will find a way. Whatever you do, DON'T GIVE UP.

You might face some rejection early on, but you need to push through. Many people I've met over the years gave up too early. They were frustrated by the barrier to entry and chose career fields that were easier to get into. Your perseverance will pay off. I can tell you from personal experience that you will not regret putting a little effort into getting a place in this amazing career field.

Some bonus tips for landing your first job as an electrician:

- Enroll in a tech or trade school as early as you can. If you go to a technical high school, that's even better.

- Be persistent and show up in person. This is still an old-school industry in a lot of respects, and meeting your future employee face-to-face will have more merit than an email or a text.

- Be mindful of your appearance and demeanor. This is a fast-paced line of work, and it can be physically demanding at times. If you show up to your interview looking tired and low energy, dragging your feet, or looking lethargic, you will not get the job.

- ⚡ *Don't* dress the part. Just because you're interviewing for a construction job doesn't mean you should show up for your interview ready to get dirty. I see a lot of guys show up dressed too casually for interviews. Although you'll never wear a dress shirt or slacks as an electrician, show up to the interview as presentable as possible.

- ⚡ Get some experience in a related trade. While looking for opportunities as an electrician, maybe you work a summer as a helper for a carpenter or plumber. Take what is available at the moment to gain some general construction experience while you work on landing your first electrical job.

- ⚡ Don't oversell yourself on your resume. Many students like to list off all the classes they've taken and tout their knowledge of switches or motor controls, but we know that you don't know anything yet. And that's okay! Focus more on your personality attributes rather than your technical skills. The technical skills will develop in time as long as you have mechanical aptitude. Sell yourself instead on your work ethic, punctuality, professionalism, problem-solving skills, or whatever other attributes you'd like to highlight.

Overall, there are plenty of things you can do to prepare yourself for a career in the skilled trades before you land your first opportunity. It may take some research, but the reward will far outweigh your early efforts. The most important thing is to persevere and not give up if you encounter obstacles early on. Remember that this is a *career* and not just a *job*. Commitment to long-term thinking will get you the ultimate reward, and some smart moves early on can pay dividends. Keep a positive mindset and show your future employers you're serious about making this a career.

CHAPTER 3

Action Items

✓ Visit your state's Department of Labor or equivalent website to learn the licensing laws in your area. How does your state's apprentice program work?

✓ Research going union vs. non-union (open shop). You can visit ibew.org and ieci.org to explore the differences.

✓ Commit to reading at least three articles and watching three videos on YouTube about getting started as an electrician. Mike Holt and Electrician U are great resources.

✓ Visit a local supply house to see if you can convince anyone to talk to you. Don't be afraid to job shadow. You might work for free for a day or two, but if it lands you an apprenticeship, it will pay you back one hundred times over. It's important to get face time with real electricians so they can remember you. This will go far beyond just being another faceless resume in an email inbox.

Chapter 4

Mastering Soft Skills

Now that we've learned about the benefits of pursuing a trade over a college career, discussed some popular misconceptions of the back-up plan, and talked about landing your first job as an apprentice, it's time to turn our focus to more actionable and applicable tips and tools for becoming an electrician. In this chapter, we'll dive into soft skills rather than technical skills. Electricians need to be well-rounded in order to be successful in a variety of situations and environments, and this chapter should help you focus on a philosophy that can be used to help you reach your full potential in this industry.

Soft skills is one of my favorite topics because soft skills are vastly underrepresented in the electrical apprenticeship education world. So, what are soft skills? The *Oxford English Dictionary* defines them as *"personal attributes that enable someone to interact effectively and harmoniously with other people."* How well can you get along with other people? So much of our education in this trade is purely technical. We often neglect the skills that back all of that up and allow you to perform effectively among coworkers, customers, and fellow tradesmen. We can recite code articles, have Ohm's Law memorized, and tell you how to reverse rotation on a motor without missing a beat. But are you a strong leader? Do you set good examples for your guys? Do you have good organizational skills that allow your projects to run smoothly? These kinds of things fall into the soft skill category that we often neglect. Here are some soft skills we can consider developing and putting effort into. Assess how you're doing with these currently and what you can do to improve.

Organization: I always go back to this because I feel it is the single most crucial aspect to master. Do you have an organizational system? Do you document your work? What apps are you using to stay organized? You may be the best at executing the physical work, but if you fail to communicate the status of your work to your foreman, superintendent, project manager, or boss, they cannot do their part to keep the job running smoothly. Do you have papers scattered all over your truck, or do you keep your files in one place? Some guys inventory their trucks every week and return their leftover stock to the supply house. Other guys throw everything in their truck for weeks on end until it's overflowing with unnecessary materials. If you spend ten minutes ripping your truck apart looking for a 2" EMT connector, do you think you'll get as much done as the guy with his parts organized in labeled bins?

Positivity: Negative people can be a cancer to the shop. Without naming names or throwing anyone under the bus, I can tell you from experience that the wrong people, with the wrong attitude, can devastate the morale of the business or job site. I've seen this both in the military and the civilian world. People are people, and no military indoctrination or corporate institutionalization can change human nature. People who chronically complain, focus on negative talk, shoot down others, and discourage younger apprentices can be detrimental. Your job is not to change these people but to make other choices for yourself. People like to commiserate, and that's fine. It's just how some people are wired. They use this to bond or to reach out for camaraderie.

You have a duty to avoid getting sucked into the culture of whining and complaining. Practice holding your head high with pride rather than participating in a complaining session with a bunch of energy vampires.

Leadership: Are you in a leadership position? Are you on a career trajectory pulling you toward an inevitable leadership position? There have been hundreds, if not thousands, of books written about leadership, so I can't even begin to scratch the surface, but I encourage you to do your own research. Although there are many different leadership styles, you have to play to your strengths. For example, I am not a particularly detail-oriented person by nature. I am very much interested in the bigger picture of things. I might have more of a hands-off leadership style when I set guys up on jobs. Where I have to be careful is where I may have *underprepared* guys. Or if I let a guy loose on a job and trust him to make good decisions, I have to be honest with myself about whether he's ready to handle the challenges that await him. Did I put him in a situation over his head? If he's capable of performing but lacks confidence, I may need to exercise some extra patience in letting him fix his mistakes rather than jumping in to save him.

Many people I've worked with over the years have an opposite leadership style. They are very detail-oriented and tend to get into the weeds. They have their own set of challenges. They might have a tendency to micromanage. Maybe they are giving too much information and not letting their guys figure out what works for them. They might be creating a culture where every single decision needs to be approved as opposed to the guys having the autonomy to make the call that they think is right for the situation. That could be restricting or inhibiting for up-and-coming electricians. Do your research and take a hard, honest look at your leadership strengths and weaknesses. At the end of the day, being a positive role model will have much more influence than any one thing.

Self-Management: How well can you manage yourself and set yourself up for success? Are you staying up too late every night because you have a new girlfriend or because you stay out drinking with your buddies? If it's causing you to be chronically late to work and drag behind everyone while living off energy drinks, it may be time to reassess your priorities. Are you eating healthy and staying hydrated? If you're eating junk food or drinking soda and suffering from constant sugar crashes, you may not be able to keep pace with the top guys on the job.

When I work on the tools, I *work*. I know a lot of top electricians that don't mess around. They work quickly, and when they strap on the tools, they are on a mission to get things done. Not prioritizing your health and wellness may affect your energy levels. If your job is to carry a 40' fiberglass extension ladder around a muddy job site that day, you may not last long at that company if you find yourself unable to keep up physically. A little self-discipline shows you know how to care for yourself and your career. I've seen eighteen-year-old kids get completely wiped out by working in a hot attic while fifty-year-old seasoned electricians work circles around them.

Time Management: How long does it take to bend a 6" offset on a piece of ¾" EMT conduit? I don't know. If you're a

CHAPTER 4

first-year apprentice, I wouldn't be surprised if you fumbled around with it for ten minutes. If you're a twenty-year veteran master electrician, I wouldn't be surprised if you could do it in under a minute. How about wiring a two-pole mechanical timer? Again, I may judge you differently based on your time in the trade and general mechanical ability. The point is, as you move along your apprenticeship, you should develop an understanding of how long a task should take to perform. If you are on a team responsible for installing two-foot troffer fixtures in a dropped ceiling, ask your foreman how many he expects you to have done by lunch. If you fall short, do some reflection on where your inefficiencies are. Maybe you notice that you got six fixtures done in the time your coworker did ten. You notice that he makes way fewer trips up and down his ladder. He packs his tool belt with everything he could need to perform that task and moves his ladder once and only once when it's time to move to the next location.

Another area where poor time management can bite you is with unnecessary trips to the truck or material storage container. Let's say you've just run out of wire nuts and need to run out to the storage trailer to replenish your stock. Look around your work area first. Are you done with that ladder? Take it back during your trip. Are there wire scraps all over the floor? Grab them before you go so you don't have to constantly walk back and forth to clean up your work area. Maybe you pass by a coworker heading to the trailer to grab materials. You ask him what he's looking for, and he replies, "Wire nuts." If you asked around before you made the trip, you could have grabbed things for the other guys so they could have stayed focused on their work areas. Never waste a trip. Clean as you go and grab things for other people. These small inefficiencies not only bleed profits, but they make you look careless and disorganized.

A little self-awareness can go a long way. Be honest with yourself and take the time to assess your soft skills periodically as you go through this journey of becoming a licensed electrician. Don't neglect the soft skills as you hammer down on the technical skills. The combination of the two sets a mediocre electrician apart from a true master.

Quick Note On Strengths And Weaknesses

We've all got strengths and weaknesses. Even the most put-together, accomplished people have blind spots, areas where they lack self-awareness. There are two ways to fix this:

- ⚡ Fix your weaknesses (very difficult)
- ⚡ Play to your strengths (very easy)

Now, don't get me wrong, you should always focus on working on your weaknesses and illuminating your blind spots, but that's a long-term play that can often take a lifetime of development and discovery. What you can take action on today is letting your strengths shine.

Here are some examples of challenges that you can choose not to let hold you back:

- ⚡ Are you having trouble understanding electrical theory? Maybe you're a slow learner but in great physical shape. Get in there and take the hard manual labor work. You can play to your strengths and build rapport with your team while you buy yourself time for more self-study and remedial education. Be the mule for a year!

CHAPTER 4

⚡ Are you too small to wrestle with heavy steel conduits? Maybe you lack height or physical strength, and these big conduit jobs are kicking your butt. Be the guy who isn't afraid to squeeze into a tight crawlspace or climb into a filthy attic. You might lack the stature to perform some of the heavier-duty work, but your team will respect you as the wiry guy who isn't afraid to jump in anywhere he's needed.

⚡ Are your people skills lacking? Maybe you're not an effective communicator and you struggle with service calls where a ton of information must be relayed to customers and coworkers. Double down on your technical skills while you slowly work on communication. You may not turn your weakness around overnight, but you can be known as a gifted troubleshooter who may have poor people skills but is an absolute genius with understanding circuitry.

Some of us were born extremely intelligent. Some of us are effective communicators with an innate ability to connect with others. Some of us have an insatiable work ethic and can persevere like no one else. All of it is a very long road. It takes a lifetime of commitment to turn your weaknesses into strengths, but it takes one decision today to double down on the gifts you already bring to your team. What can you give to others *today*?

Action Items

- ✓ Make a list of five additional soft skills I haven't listed here. Which ones do you need to work on?

- ✓ Have a friend or a family member interview you for practice. Have them assess your performance. Did you give clear, concise answers? Or did you use many filler words like "um" or "like"? Did you come across as ambitious and energetic?

- ✓ The next interaction you have with a stranger, make a point to stand tall, shake their hand firmly, and say please and thank you. Did your posture and body language make you feel any different? Practicing this can build confidence.

- ✓ Subscribe to an online magazine or email newsletter to stay current on what is happening in the electrical trade.

Chapter 5

The Down And Dirty Of Electrical Work

There will be times when a job just goes entirely off the rails. It can happen to even the best electricians, no matter how much effort you've put into planning. Things will break. Things will blow up. There will be last-minute parts that you can't get. You will drill through walls and other wiring by accident. You may get showered with asbestos, roaches, or rat droppings from a falling ceiling. A million things can happen. The important thing is to commit to seeing the project through. If you end up in one of these unfortunate situations, the only thing you can do is remain calm and take it to the finish line. No one is going to step in and save you. You'll need some grit and discipline to persevere through the situation. Some examples of things that can go wrong include:

⚡ You're replacing a large piece of equipment in a commercial building, and you absolutely cannot leave until the power is back on. This project has been planned for weeks, and a lot of people have put their faith in you (or your team) to pull this off. You find out mid-way through that you're missing parts, you didn't plan properly, there was a factory defect, you're moving more slowly than you anticipated, the wiring doesn't fit into the lugs or enclosure, or a host of other issues. You may get stuck on that job for twelve hours straight working overnight, but you HAVE TO finish and get the power back on.

⚡ You're disassembling a complicated section of wiring, and you think you have a grasp on it. After ripping everything out, you realize you mislabeled some of the wiring or did not take sufficient notes. You've got a rat's nest on your hands. It's already 5:00 p.m., and the homeowners have a crying baby.

⚡ Your day is packed with service calls. You're doing a lot of small "hit and run" repair jobs. Your boss has scheduled you for three stops today. The schedule looked reasonable, but you ran into unexpected issues on the first stop, and you've already been there for four hours.

⚡ You're installing large, complicated chandeliers at a new storefront. They're very challenging and heavy. You're on a tall ladder, and it's awkward, but you've managed to move through three of them so far. When you're on your way to starting the fourth one, you realize you misinterpreted the plans and installed them in the wrong locations. The general contractor throws a fit when you tell him you're going to have to rework everything because the store is scheduled for a grand opening tomorrow morning.

CHAPTER 5

⚡ You're installing recessed lighting in a high-end home. You've carefully taped off the entryways for dust control and installed drop cloths everywhere to protect the flooring. You're drilling into the ceiling for the last light, and since everything has been going so well, you don't look too carefully. You neglected the fact that you're working in a living room that's directly under a bathroom. You've drilled under the shower pan right through the drain pipe. Dirty water comes pouring through the ceiling of this $2 million house as your boss and the homeowner watch in horror.

The nature of electrical work can often be unpredictable. You're dealing with many moving parts, and many unknown variables are at play, whether it be aging equipment or difficult people. While it's often not easy and sometimes downright frustrating, the reward of conquering a challenge always feels amazing, and you'll be glad you stuck with it to the end. Imagine exhaustively pursuing a wiring issue that two electricians before you gave up on. You work through it for a few hours and then notice something the other two guys missed. You make some adjustments, and voila! The power is back on, and you're the hero of the day. Moments like these can be enriching and encouraging. I highly suggest that you pursue challenges like this to make you a better electrician and put yourself in situations that deepen your love and respect for this trade.

The bad news is that things WILL GO WRONG. The good news is that what determines your success in this industry will all be in the recovery. You must remember that everyone who came before you has had brutally difficult days, but we stuck with it. You will push through to the other side and be forced to think on your feet. But you will always find a way through it.

Aside from the daily challenges of electrical work's unpredictable nature, there are also working conditions that are less than desirable at times. I've worked on picturesque golf courses overlooking the ocean, rental cabins in the woods, and high-end office buildings with every amenity you could ask for. Unfortunately, on the other side of that same coin, I've also worked in filthy crawl spaces full of asbestos and dead rats and underground manholes filled with freezing water or infested by spiders. It's certainly not for everyone, but if you're tough enough, here are some of the realities you should be aware of and ready to handle:

- *Heights:* You may spend hours on the top of a forty-foot extension ladder replacing flood lights or on a steep roof with a body harness tied to a chimney. I've even had to do a service call on the top of the Empire State Building. (If you're scared of heights, I highly recommend against taking a job like that!) You may also work off the platform of a bucket truck or aerial lift sixty-five feet in the air that swings violently every time you shift your weight, so consider your ability to handle motion sickness as well.

- *Dirty environments:* A lot of wiring I've done over the years on both the commercial and residential sides involved crawling through crawlspaces to get under a building. I'll never forget the first crawlspace I went in. It was under a radio station in New Jersey. My boss handed me a large Mag-Light flashlight and told me to use it to beat off the rats that might come for me! That scenario did not come to fruition that day, but there are other hazards to be aware of. Some older buildings can be contaminated with leaky sewer pipes, asbestos, or other airborne contaminants. Always wear a mask to protect your lungs.

CHAPTER 5

- ⚡ *Extreme heat/cold:* Electrical work can be performed inside or outside, and we work all year, so be sure you're prepared for anything. You might spend your entire winter putting up parking lot lights in ten-degree weather. Conversely, you might spend a week in August installing a large motor control cabinet on the mezzanine above a steel mill in 120-degree temperatures. Sometimes, we get to work outside on beautiful summer days, but with that also comes working in the snow or rain and doing whatever it takes to get the job done. Always come to work prepared with rain gear, cold weather gear, and water.

- ⚡ *Underground work:* A good portion of the work you'll do in the early stages of a new building will involve placing all of the underground utilities in the ground. This can involve climbing in and out of muddy trenches all day. Some areas may have high water tables where you may jump into a vault only to realize you're now standing in two feet of ice-cold water and you're soaked through your boots. You'll have to finish your day out in wet socks, and there isn't much you can do. There also may be times when it begins to downpour, and you're covered in mud from head to toe. Think about what protection you might want to keep in your car to avoid ruining your seats.

- ⚡ *General safety concerns:* You'll be exposed to high voltages on a constant basis. If you do commercial or industrial work or work on a utility line crew, you may even be exposed to fatally high voltages that can kill you if not approached properly. You'll receive extensive safety training on how to approach a variety of situations safely, ensuring you go home to your family each night. There are also many haphazard safety concerns that don't exactly fit into any one category. For example, I've been splashed with battery acid, had equipment dropped on my head from six feet above me, and almost had my hand crushed by a misfiring hydraulic press. Please use situational awareness at all times, and don't take your safety training lightly. If you feel that your company is not providing the appropriate equipment or level of training, please ask your boss to clarify safe practices and provide the appropriate training.

As much as I would encourage you to be aware of the undesirable environments you may find yourself in, I'd like to equally encourage you not to be intimidated by this. As I've said, this is not an office job and is not for everyone, but don't be discouraged! Working in these challenging environments can be extremely fun. You'll have stories to tell your friends and family they won't even believe. I still get asked at parties to retell old electrical stories that sound dangerous and adventurous to today's average office dweller. As long as you prioritize your safety and the safety of your wingmen, you can have some of the best times of your working life in these situations. Not everyone is up for it, but if you think you are, we want you in our trade.

CHAPTER 5

Action Items

✓ If you've never worked a day in any sort of construction or physical trade, find a temporary labor agency that will get you some experience, even if it's just mixing cement, demolishing an old building, or loading a dumpster. It will give you an honest look into whether you see yourself in this line of work.

✓ Write out your ideal job. What does a perfect day look like for you? Are you working outside or inside? What kind of work are you doing? Are you working alone or in a team? The more detail and the more you daydream, the better.

✓ Are you cool under pressure? Jot down a few paragraphs about a time when something didn't go your way. How did you handle it? What did you do about it?

✓ Inventory your gear. Are you ready to work? Do you own good cold-weather gear, rain gear, a lunchbox, and a cooler? Make sure your cold-weather gear includes a wool hat and thin and thick gloves. You'll sometimes need thin gloves for working with small parts.

Chapter 6

The Electrical Trade As A Path To Entrepreneurship

I've talked with many people who see the skilled trades as a pathway to entrepreneurship. Many young people dream of being their own boss. They see themselves running a small construction company and calling the shots. Some may even have larger aspirations and see themselves scaling up a service business that will eventually employ an entire team of electricians. Regardless of your vision, the skilled trades are a viable path to self-employment.

I would highly suggest you do some research on the rules in your home state. What level of schooling and licensing is required? How much and what type of insurance will you be required to carry? What are the rules for hiring employees? Will you need to be bonded? The answers to these questions will vary greatly depending on your location and target market. However, I'd be willing to bet that almost every state has made these requirements widely accessible. It just may take a little bit of research.

Becoming self-employed can be extremely rewarding. You can set your own schedule. You can do things your way. I know many "one-man shows" that are such perfectionists that they don't want to work with others. Going into business has allowed them the freedom to pursue that higher quality level of work on their own. Some people feel like they can make more money, while some just want the freedom of self-employment. No matter your motive, there is ample opportunity to make this a reality.

One caution, though: don't rush into it too soon in your career. There is an epidemic of young, confident electricians who think they know more than they do. When you go out into your own business, you can't just call your boss anytime you get into a pinch. You can easily get in over your head and lose serious amounts of money if you mess up. Your particular state may only require four years of experience to become a licensed electrical contractor, but you may not have accumulated enough of the skills that will allow you to thrive as a business owner. I would make sure you've done a variety of projects throughout both the residential and commercial worlds. Also, make sure you gain some sort of business knowledge before you go out and get hurt financially. Understanding some basic principles of accounting, contracts, and managing your money will go a very long way.

Here are some actionable steps for becoming a licensed electrical contractor:

- ⚡ Complete your apprenticeship program.
- ⚡ Obtain your electrician license.
- ⚡ Research the requirements in your state on what it takes to become a licensed electrical contractor. For example, in Connecticut, you must work a total

CHAPTER 6

of twelve thousand verifiable hours to become a licensed electrical contractor. This consists of eight thousand hours to obtain a journeyman electrician license and an additional four thousand hours for your electrical contractor's license, which will require you to pass a code and theory exam and a basic business exam. Check with your state's rules for licensing requirements in your area.

- ⚡ Study for your exams. You would think this goes without saying, but you'd be surprised by how many people show up completely unprepared for one of the most life-changing days of their lives.

- ⚡ Get your insurance in place. You'll need liability insurance at a bare minimum. You'll also need worker's compensation insurance if you plan to have employees. If you plan to pursue municipal or federal contracts, you may also need a performance or bid bond, sometimes called a P&P bond.

- ⚡ Get a vehicle. Don't forget to add a commercial auto policy to that list of insurances.

- ⚡ Get your vehicle fitted out. Don't forget an empty van or pickup truck is only the beginning, and it's not enough to keep you stocked and organized. You'll need ladder racks, tool and storage boxes, hand tools, power tools, and other truck accessories.

- ⚡ Find a graphic designer. Will you have your truck lettered with your company name? Will you have a logo that you'll use on your truck, email signature, and invoices? If so, you'll want that done professionally.

- ⚡ Get an accountant and a bookkeeping system in place. You want to have that lined up *before* you start making money. Trust me, you will not want to go back through your first year's finances trying to make sense of it when taxes are due. You'll be thankful that you've implemented a system early in your business.

⚡ Register your business. Once you've decided on a name, you'll need this business to exist on paper. You'll need a federal employer identification number (FEIN), which is like a social security number for your business. You'll use this quarterly and annually to file taxes. You may also need a state registration or tax ID number (again, check with your local regulations). You must also decide how you plan to structure your business entity. Will you be a limited liability company (LLC)? Will you incorporate? I will not go into any detail here because each business structure has different rules concerning tax liabilities. I would highly recommend you do your research on this before making a decision.

⚡ Develop a marketing strategy. How will you get business? Will you work directly for homeowners, or will you work as a subcontractor for general contractors? Will you pursue residential, commercial, or industrial projects? How will you get yourself in front of these people? You might consider making a website and paying for search engine optimization or Google AdWords. Maybe you already have some good connections but need to rekindle those relationships. If you want to pursue new construction, how do you get on the bid list of contractors and developers? There are a lot of considerations to think about here, and we can devote an entire book to this. I would suggest doing your own research and reading up on marketing.

⚡ Establish a line of credit. Hopefully, you've been building credit since you graduated high school and now have an impeccable credit score. Go to your bank and establish a line of credit NOW. You'll need credit if you ever decide to grow. The bank will be happy to talk to you when you look good on paper, so it's important to establish this early. Don't go into the bank after a job has gone wrong and you're now in debt to several people. The bank will dismiss you or charge you credit terms that make any new debt unsustainable. Develop a good relationship with your banker. Discuss whatever assets you may be able to use as collateral and establish a line of credit with fair terms.

⚡ Establish accounts at all of your local supply houses. They may ask for a financial statement to make sure they're doing business with a trustworthy person. (Again, see why building good credit early in life is crucial?!) Your ability to quickly procure supplies at a reasonable price will make or break your business, so establish a credit account and treat your vendors well.

⚡ Implement a pricing formula. Many contractors charge what they think is the "going rate" only to discover they are undercharging and at risk of going bankrupt. You need to take a hard look at your expenses and charge accordingly. How much do all of your expenses add up to a month? How many billable hours can you book each month? Don't forget that not every hour of your day is billable time. You may work forty hours on your tools, but when do you plan on paying bills, dealing with insurance companies, writing estimates, invoicing completed work, ordering materials, marketing yourself, attending walkthroughs and meetings, and many of the other tasks required of you? Here is a simple formula you can use:

> ⚡ Let's say you plan to work thirty hours a week of billable time and twenty hours a week on administrative and ancillary tasks like those we've previously discussed. Let's assume you plan to take

two weeks off every year to spend time with family around the holidays and for a week in the summer. This leaves you with 1,500 working hours every year. That assumes that you never take a single sick day because you take care of yourself. Here is how you figure out your minimum break-even rate:

→ Total annual expenses divided by number of billable hours worked per year.

So, in our example, although you spend fifty hours a week working, you'll only bill for thirty of these hours. The annual expenses of running a business will vary depending on the size of your business. Mine fluctuated between $200,000 and $600,000 per year as I hired and fired employees. Let's say you are just starting out, and your first year will cost $125,000:

Total annual expenses ($125,000) divided by number of billable hours worked (1,500) = $83.33 per hour.

So, in this case, $83.33 is your *break-even* hourly rate. That means you will have a profit of exactly $0 at the end of the year if you charge $83.33. Of course, you will be out of business very quickly if you charge that, so you'll need to make a profit. Here is what your billable hourly rate would look like at different profit margins:

10% profit margin: $91.66 hourly rate
15% profit margin: $95.83 hourly rate
25% profit margin: $104.16 hourly rate

At a 10% margin, you would make $12,500 for yourself at the end of the year if you executed your plan perfectly. At a 25% margin, you would make $31,250 at the end of the year. Only you know what you need to live on, but if you're not profiting $100,000 plus per year, there is no point in going into business for yourself unless you truly crave the freedom.

Key Tips

⚡ Take care of yourself. If you want to chase the dream and work one hundred hours per week, go for it! Just don't forget that you're human. You need sleep, water, and proper nutrition.

⚡ Don't burn out. Taking on too much work can produce a lot of stress and make you hate the career you once loved.

⚡ Make good hiring decisions. One of the best pieces of advice I got when it comes to employees is that you should be "slow to hire but quick to fire." Don't tolerate nonsense from people who are supposed to be representing you in a positive light.

⚡ Don't forget to save. Many people who work for other companies have a company 401k that they can contribute to in order to save for retirement. For reasons I'll never understand, many people forget to establish a retirement savings plan for themselves once they go into business. There are several good investment options for self-employed individuals, such as individual retirement accounts (IRAs). I would suggest you talk to a financial advisor. Just because you own the company now doesn't mean you'll work until the day you die.

⚡ Use your business to buy real estate. Instead of leasing the office we operated out of, I decided to purchase it.

Since then, it has doubled in value and turned out to be one of my best moves. I also purchased fixer-upper homes and renovated them along the way, improving their value and providing opportunities for other contractors and lovely homes for future tenants. Many tradesmen I know are involved in real estate investing in one capacity or another. Our ability to perform the work ourselves and our deep knowledge of the residential and commercial real estate markets put us on a unique path to capitalize on opportunities that may not be available to the general public. You may get a good off-market deal or be asked to buy into a business you're helping renovate. I highly encourage you to research real estate and add it to your repertoire and investment portfolio as you build your career.

⚡ Practice the golden rule. What goes around comes around. Karma. Do unto others as you would have done. These ideas are reiterated through every culture and religion, but there is a good reason for that. The electrical contracting world is fairly small, and you will quickly find yourself setting a reputation. Work hard to make sure it's a good one. Be fair to customers, vendors, employees, and others, and your work will be rewarded. Remember that bad news travels faster than good news, and people have very good memories when they've been treated unfairly.

⚡ Never stop building your network. Remember those people you called when you started your business to get things off the ground? Well, that never ends. Your network of business owners, homeowners, other contractors, and vendors will be instrumental in allowing you to start and grow your business. Always remain gracious to those who helped you along the way. Sending a handwritten thank you note or buying someone lunch can go a long way.

- ⚡ Practice humility. You're going to make some foolish mistakes at the beginning of your business, just like you made some foolish mistakes during the first few years of your apprenticeship. This is part of the learning process. Don't beat yourself up, but at the same time, continue to hold yourself to high standards to avoid making costly mistakes in the future.

- ⚡ Listen to your gut. If something doesn't seem right, it isn't. Not everyone will be eager to help you. There will be homeowners and general contractors who hire you with no intention to ever pay you. They assume you're young, new in business, and won't pursue legal actions if screwed over. These are dishonest people who prey on new contractors. Don't be afraid to walk away from a job before it starts. I once ripped a contract up in front of a customer because the red flags began to emerge. Be cautious and protect yourself against dishonest people. That also includes employees who may steal from you.

- ⚡ The last and final suggestion I would make is to set realistic expectations. Running a business can be extremely stressful and time-consuming, so make sure you have the right passion, attitude, and work ethic to deal with what's ahead. It can be extremely rewarding at times, and there is no limit to what you can make. For example, if you find yourself in a niche within the industry where all of your peers are charging low margins, and you are constantly being undercut, you may move over to a more specialized side of the industry where a margin upwards of 50 percent is commonplace. If you can dream it, you can do it, but not without sacrifice and long-term thinking.

Don't forget very few business owners work forty hours per week. You may get to that point eventually, but please plan for the worst. In my first two years of business, eighty-hour weeks were not uncommon. I even remember a few weeks where I clocked in over one hundred hours! I remember my wife bringing me dinner at a factory we were finishing wiring so that I could stay there all night working without having to go home! Of course, once you get established and begin to understand how your business operates on a deeper level, you can begin to scale back and gain more control. Most importantly, you're enjoying it and not letting it run your life.

Remember, you run a business; the business does not run you. Don't be afraid to establish boundaries with customers and employees because you are ultimately in control. The electrical trade is not for everyone, and the subset of people that make it all the way to being electrical contractors is even fewer. If you think you have what it takes, then the best thing you can do is jump in with both feet and commit to becoming as profitable as you can, as quickly as you can. Good luck!

Surprises

As I write this, I'm getting close to celebrating my twentieth year in this amazing trade. Here are some surprises I've learned along the way.

- ⚡ Good electricians are often extremely intelligent people
- ⚡ There are niches within niches that you wouldn't even know about until you get into this. (Ever heard of a SCADA system?)

CHAPTER 6

- ⚡ Commercial, residential, and industrial wiring all come with unique challenges and opportunities

- ⚡ Most electricians are very proud of their work and often brag about how neat their electrical work is—how accurately they can snake a wire through a wall or the beauty and precision of their conduit bending.

- ⚡ The money can be better than you ever thought if you work hard at the right opportunities.

- ⚡ You'll hear some highly entertaining stories from old-time electricians.

- ⚡ The average electrician is close to retirement age.

- ⚡ This industry is full of interesting and passionate people.

- ⚡ There is an entire industry of non-electricians around us, such as lighting reps, designers, drafters, engineers, and switchgear specialists.

- ⚡ Electrical work can be extremely dangerous, so always respect it and use situational awareness.

- ⚡ There is a camaraderie in the electrical trade, and you'll often spend hours sharing stories with other electricians.

- ⚡ We don't call ourselves sparkies, but other trades call us that.

- ⚡ A good troubleshooter is worth his weight in gold.

- ⚡ This trade will expose you to all sorts of personality types, some of which are *rough*. Take the good with the bad.

- ⚡ The best way to learn is by doing, but the best electricians are the ones who deeply understand theory on top of practice.

Action Items

✓ Have you ever seen yourself owning a business? What kind of business would it be? What would you call it? Would you be the sole proprietor or grow it into a large team?

✓ Just like you did with licensing laws earlier, do some research on becoming an electrical contractor in your state.

✓ Ask your friends and family to see if anyone knows a business owner, even if it's in an unrelated field. Can you convince that person to give you ten minutes of their time to share their experience with you?

✓ Develop a savings plan if this is something you're serious about. When will you go into business? How much money will you need to spend in the first year? How much do you need to begin saving per year to be ready for that day?

Chapter 7

Creating Your Own Luck
(The Tale Of Two Electricians)

The electrical trade is no different than any other industry in the sense that your success depends on you creating your own luck. Whichever career field you pursue, there will be opportunities, choices, and challenges. This is universal across all trades; much of it is just learning to navigate life as we grow and mature. However, there are some ideas that we can apply specifically to the electrical trade. The opportunity of a lifetime might be right in front of your face, but if you're not in the frame of mind to capitalize on it, that opportunity will pass you by. The sooner you establish a track record of making good decisions, the sooner that series of good decisions will compound and begin to pay dividends in your life. Let's look at the stories of John and Steve to see how this could play out in the real world.

John and Steve are high school friends. They are both good with their hands and mechanically inclined. They've been considering all the skilled trades as viable career paths, and their parents support that path as a long-term future. After attending a local job fair and speaking with plumbing, HVAC, welding, construction management, masonry, and electrical professionals, they're blown away by the electrician's stories. The variety and diversity of work, the knowledge of how they interact with the other trades, the opportunity to apply the added mental challenge of troubleshooting—this is it! The electrician seems cool and confident. He's got an energy about him that makes John and Steve think he's the real deal. "We have to become electricians," they agree as they leave the fair.

After graduation, they are determined to find summer jobs as helpers and go out and pound the pavement. They research local companies online and call the electrician they met back at the job fair for advice. Although they strike out a lot at first (most companies are only looking for already licensed guys), they persist. They even take pictures of the sides of electrical vans when they see them drive by; any lead will do!

After two weeks, Steve is ready to give up. They've called and emailed over a dozen companies at this point, and they're getting nowhere. "What happened to all the opportunities allegedly available in electrical?" he wonders. The companies want someone who already has a license. If not, they want someone who at least has some registered apprentice hours, which seems like a catch-22. "Maybe it isn't like what people say; maybe we just go to college like all our friends are doing and forget about it," Steve ponders in exasperation. But John is determined. "Remember how many opportunities we learned about at that career fair? This might be slow going, but we have to think long-term. All we have to do is land the first opportunity, and then from there, we're in!"

CHAPTER 7

In a stroke of serendipity, John and Steve are driving by an electrical supply house later that day. The parking lot is full of electrical trucks with different company logos. It seems very busy. People are hustling in and out, pushing carts full of materials and stocking their vans. They see some of the company names they've heard of before but also some new names they don't recognize. They're surprised how many of these companies didn't appear in their Google search. "How do all of these companies stay in business and get customers if they don't even have an online listing or a website?" they wonder. Some vans don't even have a phone number on the side! They can't believe it.

"Maybe there are more companies out there than we realized," says John. "Let's go in there and see if anyone is hiring. Instead of hunting down all these different companies one by one, we can cast a wide net and get them all in one place."

Steve is a little hesitant to go in. "Look at these guys. Some of them look rough. We're just kids. We're just going to bother them. Let's just forget about it." John agrees that some of the guys are rough-looking. There are a lot of beards and tattoos. Most of the guys are a lot older and look grumpy and ornery. The younger guys are moving quickly and don't even notice the two kids in the parking lot as they quickly toss their materials into the van and speed off.

"Let's just go for it," John insists. "If we really want to be electricians, we can't leave any stone unturned." Steve reluctantly agrees, and they walk into the supply house. There are about eight electricians scattered around what looks like maybe three or four lines. It's hard to tell because the whole system seems a little chaotic. "Jimmy, you all set?" one of the employees behind the counter yells out. An older guy standing with his arms folded gives him a half wave with one hand, indicating he's already been helped. "Okay, who's next? Young guns there, step up, whaddya need?" he says as he gestures John and Steve up to the counter. He grabs a pen and a pad of paper and looks down at it as if to expect them to start firing an order off at him.

"We're not actually here to buy anything today. My friend and I have just graduated high school, and we're looking to get started in electrical. We figured you guys might know if one of your regular customers is hiring?" "

Yeah, everybody is hiring if you got a license," the guy retorts. "You guys know anyone hiring green apprentices?" he casts out to the three or four guys standing around his counter sections. "You guys have resumes?" one of the electricians asks the kids.

"Well, no, we don't, but we can get them," John answers sheepishly. "We really don't have any experience. We worked some odd jobs here and there doing landscaping and bagging groceries senior year, but that's about it." The electrician seems intrigued by their resourcefulness and candor.

"Follow me outside. I think I saw Mike from Green Electric here when I came in. Let's see if I can catch him." The kids follow him outside to a van at the end of the row with the Green Electric LLC lettering. "Yo Mike, how are you, man?" he yells to a guy who is just finishing loading his new materials into the van. He's got a few bundles of shiny aluminum pipe and a bunch of different boxes of all kinds of fittings that the kids have never seen before. John and Steve quickly think they might be in over their heads. What is all this stuff?

"Hey buddy, we're slammed right now. It's gonna be a busy summer. Same old story: can't find good guys willing to work. All these young apprentices think they're going to stand around and make journeyman money after the first two weeks."

CHAPTER 7

"Well, these two kids here are looking for work. Good luck, boys," the other electrician says as he turns to head back inside.

"Oh, so you guys are looking for work. That's good because we need guys," Mike says. "Your timing is actually pretty decent because we have a big job starting on Monday down in Franklin, and we're looking for some help. You guys don't look licensed," Mike says suspiciously. John gives him the whole lowdown he gave the counter guy, and Mike's demeanor stays unchanged.

"Well, we're really looking for licensed guys, but we can use any help we can get for now. We might have some apprentice slots coming up soon, but for now, I could use some help with grunt work. We need some trenches dug. You guys can load dumpsters and unload delivery trucks. That sounds like something you can do?"

"Yes, sir, absolutely," they blurt out instinctively. "We'll take any opportunity we can get. We're eager to get started".

"Alright, fair enough. We'll see what you're made out of," Mike replies. "You seem like pretty good kids. Give me one of your phone numbers, and I'll text you the address. We start there on Monday at 6:30 a.m. Bring basic hand tools if you have them, some good gloves, we'll figure out the rest later. Sound good?"

John and Steve shake hands with Mike and head back into their car. "Man, Franklin is a LONG way away. Plus, the traffic going that way in the morning can be brutal. I don't know if we should have taken this job," Steve says with a mix of concern and regret.

"Steve, we've been looking for weeks now, and this opportunity practically fell into our laps. Yeah, it's far, and there is traffic that way, but don't forget he says it's a 6:30 start time. We'll be on the road at 5:15 at the latest, and the highway will be wide open. This is our chance. We have to give this a shot. What if this works out and the next job is right in town for us?" John retorts.

"Okay, John, I guess you're right. I still don't know, but I'll try it. I mean, he didn't even mention if we get gas money or anything. You know my truck isn't good on gas.".

"Don't worry about that. It's a small investment in your future. We told Mike we'd be there and this is our shot".

That Sunday, all of John and Steve's friends are celebrating their high school graduation at a big bonfire. As the night winds on, there is no sign of the party slowing down. Everyone is in good spirits, talking about their plans for after high school and telling stories about their high school years. John checks the time and notices it's getting late. "Hey Steve, I'm gonna split. Remember, tomorrow morning is our big day to kick that job off."

"Oh man, that's right. Yeah, I'll be fine. I'll catch up with you later. I'm having too much fun. There are still more people here I haven't even had a chance to talk to yet," Steve replies, half distracted with a freshly opened beer in his hand.

John takes off to get ready for the next day. He puts together what he can of a basic tool bag. He has some decent tools from taking shop class back in school, but he also has some old stuff still hanging around from his grandfather's tool collection. He doesn't even know what some of the stuff is, but he figures he might as well bring it. He throws a basic collection of screwdrivers, pliers, a hammer, tape measure, and some of the mysterious tools in a backpack and tosses it into his trunk for the morning. Mike also mentioned that they'd be digging some trenches. John remembers doing some trench work for an irrigation line while helping a landscaper last summer. That work was no joke with the rocky soil they have around here, so he knows he's in for a challenge.

CHAPTER 7

He fills up some water bottles and puts a lunch together for tomorrow. That night, he lies in bed daydreaming about this new opportunity. How much will they learn tomorrow? What exactly will they be working on? If I work hard enough and leave a good impression on Mike, can this turn into an apprenticeship? If I get started on my hours now when I'm seventeen, I'll be a licensed journeyman making six figures at twenty-one! My friends will still be in college, living off Mom and Dad while I'm shopping for my first house!" He dozes off among the endless possibilities swirling around his head, ready for whatever tomorrow brings.

The alarm startles John awake at 4:45. "Man, it's ridiculously early," he thinks. He's only been up this early one time in his entire life when his family had to catch an early flight across the country to visit his aunt. "Can I do this every day?" he wonders briefly while he fumbles in the dark for the alarm. He texts Steve to confirm the plan. They were going to carpool down there together to save on gas.

He packs up the water and lunch he set aside last night while he waits for Steve's response. It's 5:05 now, and still nothing. He gives Steve a call, which goes straight to a voicemail box that hasn't been set up yet. He fires off another text telling Steve they have to get on the road.

John's got three minutes to hit the road, and he's getting nervous now. This opportunity means a lot to him. They've been talking about it for weeks, and he doesn't want to mess this up. He knows how hard it was to find someone willing to take on an unlicensed guy. At the same time, he's loyal to Steve. They've been in the same classes since seventh grade, and he would never want to leave him hanging. Five-fifteen rolls around, and it's still radio silence. "I hope you make it, but I gotta go!" John thinks to himself as he pulls out of the neighborhood and heads towards the highway.

He pulls up to the address Mike gave him with plenty of time to spare. It's 6:11, and he's surprised at how much traffic is already on the road. "This many people are already out there this early?" he wonders. The jobsite is a large farmhouse colonial on a decent-sized lot. The place is nice, but it definitely needs some work. There is a classic dark red barn behind the property with a few machines next to it that John doesn't recognize.

He sees Mike's electrical van parked at the end of the driveway and heads that way. Mike is standing next to the open side doors of the van with a tall, skinny guy wearing the same company shirt. "Wow, you passed the first test: you made it to work on time," Mike says sarcastically. "Where's your buddy?"

"I haven't heard from him; maybe he had car trouble," John answers.

Mike and the other electrician look at each other and laugh. "Yeah, car trouble. That's about the sixth time this month we've heard that one. Cars must be getting more and more unreliable. Hey Sam, did you ever miss work for *car trouble* when you were starting out?"

"You know, now that I think of it, I guess I was pretty lucky. I must have had a really good car," Sam responds jokingly.

"So anyway, kid, this is Sam. You'll be working with both of us today. Sam's still an apprentice, but he knows his stuff. Sam, when do you take your journeyman exam again?"

"Well, I've got about two hundred hours left until I can register, so I figure I'll be licensed by the end of the summer for sure." Sam doesn't seem that much older than John, but he has this quiet confidence. John is impressed and hopes to get himself into a position like that as soon as possible.

CHAPTER 7

"Well, since you're doing a lot of digging today, I assume you brought some good gloves?" Mike says.

John feels a little embarrassed. He really felt like he'd thought of everything. "Uh, no sir, I brought my hand tools," he responds with a little reservation.

"Well, you won't be needing those right away. You're going to get this trench open for us, so if you don't have gloves, I hope you got tough hands," Mike responds. "Alright, let's go, boys. Get this trench started before it gets too damn hot today. You ever run a trencher?" Mike asks.

Run a trencher? John thinks to himself. *I've never even heard of a trencher.* "Um, well, no, I haven't," he replies.

"Um, well, today you will," Mike responds mockingly. He has a sharp wit but doesn't seem like the kind of guy who wants to cut you down. He seems like he's all business but tries to throw in a few comments here and there, mostly for Sam's entertainment.

"So the ground up here is pretty rocky, and we've got to get a trench from the main house to the garage. The guy who bought the house fixes up cars, so he wants this barn wired up with lights, a hydraulic lift, and some other stuff, but don't worry about that. You just stay focused on digging. Sam's gonna show you how to run the trencher, but you've gotta go easy. Since the ground is so damn rocky, she can stall out if you go too fast and start hitting rock. That's what the pickax is for. Drop the blade slowly and get a feel for it. Always walk backwards, and if you feel the motor bogging down, let up on it. If we have some high spots, you'll get those by hand. Sam's going to get you set up. I'll be in that main house." Mike grabs his tools and marches off.

Sam fires up the trenching machine through a simple process of a few buttons and knobs and gets it running. "This is how you drop the blade!" he yells over the idling motor

97

as he points the controls out to John. "Remember, ALWAYS walk backwards and feel out the machine. Let it do the work". Sam does a quick demonstration and hands it off to John. "There's nothing to it. Nice and straight, follow that painted line."

John is a little hesitant for a split second. He's been in the electrical trade for about fifteen minutes now. Is he qualified to do this? He shrugs off his nerves and gets to work. The machine feels a lot heavier than it looked when Sam was running it, and he's having a little trouble staying on course, but he keeps it going and, after a few false starts, begins to get the hang of it.

Meanwhile, Steve is out on the street looking for the jobsite. He's called John three times, but there is no chance of him hearing his phone ring over the roar of the trenching machine. Steve parks on the street because the driveway is now full of vans and trucks. He's the last one there, so framers, roofers, plumbers, electricians, and HVAC techs are already on site. The work is in full swing, and the scene is a little chaotic. The roofers yell down to the helpers, and the framers yell measurements at each other over the buzz of a circular saw. Steve wanders into the main house with uncertainty, hoping to spot John. A plumber on his way back out to his van almost knocks him over. "Watch where the hell you're walking, kid. You're not at your mommy's house anymore," he sneers as he breezes by faster than Steve could even retort.

As he wanders the house, peeking into every room, he hears a familiar voice shout out over the clatter of the jobsite. "Whoa, sleeping beauty! I'm glad you've graced us with your presence, princess." He turns around to see Mike with a huge drill in his hand covered in wood splinters. Steve turns a little red, but he wouldn't be crazy enough to backtalk

CHAPTER 7

Mike. "Go out back to the barn to help your buddy. He's already set up."

Steve asks where the barn is, but Mike goes back to drilling wood studs out so quickly that he doesn't even hear Steve's timid response over the whirl of the drill. Steve saunters out through the back door and gets hit with the late morning sun. It's getting seriously hot now, and his mind flashes to the fact that he hasn't brought any food or water with him because of waking up late. He sees John out by the barn and waves to him, but John is intensely watching the trenching blade as he clumsily pulls the machine around.

Sam notices Steve and intercepts him before he makes it out to John. "You must be the new helper. I hope you got your beauty rest. Go help your boy. There's a pickaxe there leaning against the barn. You can hack away at the rocks and roots so he can stay on the machine," Sam orders. Steve doesn't even know what that means. He's lost and embarrassed and considers just turning around and leaving. But he sucks it up and gets John's attention. John gives him the low down on what they're working on, and they get back to work.

After a few hours in the hot sun, Sam comes out waving them down, moving his hand across his neck as if to signal "kill the machine." John fumbles for the kill switch and finds it after a few tries. The machine sputters to a halt, and for the first time, the environment seems peaceful and serene.

"You guys can break if you want. Get some shade in the barn and stay hydrated. Hope you brought lunch because there's really not much out here except a gas station about two miles that way."

"We're good, Sam, thanks," John replies, wiping sweat from his forehead with the back of a dirty glove he borrowed from Mike. They head into the barn to get some shade and rehydrate. They find two old crates to turn over and sit down in the dusty barn. John brings out a cooler and a large thermos full of water that he starts guzzling down.

"Man, I didn't bring anything. I didn't realize it was gonna be this hot," Steve admits.

"Yeah, it's the first week of July, ya know? It gets hot in July," John replies sarcastically. "Here, I brought another bottle of water, and we can split this bag of trail mix."

They settle in and start to take their break. They bicker a little about Steve almost missing his first day, but they try to keep it down so as not to embarrass themselves too much. About fifteen minutes go by, and the cool shade feels great. They notice that Sam hasn't stopped to eat and that he's run back into the barn twice to grab a handful of gray plastic pieces out of a bin.

"Hey Sam, you don't eat lunch?" John yells out before Sam has a chance to march back out into the sun.

"Nah, I'm good boys. I don't usually eat. I get into a rhythm and don't like to slow down my roll, but you guys go ahead. Take your break; you get thirty minutes."

Steve doesn't react, but John gets up off his crate. "I'm going to go see what Sam's working on. You wanna go check it out?" he offers to Steve.

"What are you? Teacher's pet?" Steve cuts back.

"No, man, this is our chance to see some real electrical work. Let's see what he's working on."

"I'm good. He said we get a half hour, I'm taking it. Plus, I'm dead from last night. This shade feels good," Steve mutters while he tosses another handful of trail mix into his mouth, not budging.

CHAPTER 7

"Okay, suit yourself, man," John replies as he grabs his gloves and shoots back out of the barn.

He sees Sam not far from where they were working. He's kneeling in the grass on one knee, cutting a piece of gray pipe with some kind of weird-looking saw that John doesn't recognize. "Hey Sam, excuse me, I don't want to bother you. I just was curious to see what you're working on."

"Yeah, sure thing, man," Sam happily replies, seeming mildly impressed with John's level of interest. "I'm cutting up some PVC conduit. This is what we're going to run through that trench when you guys are done. And this is a band saw," he motions to the saw that John couldn't identify. "You can use a Sawzall too, but this thing has a really fine blade, and you get a nice cut. Gives you a little more control, ya know?" Sam says rhetorically. "We gotta finish this trench so we can get this pipe in the ground. Once it's all set, we'll pull the wires through from the main house so we can feed the barn and put in a nice little twelve-circuit sub-panel."

John has no idea what Sam's talking about, but he nods in agreement, grateful to be talking to a "real" electrician. "I really want to have everything pulled in by Wednesday midday, so you guys just keep going with that trench the way you're going. Once you get that first pass in, I have another pickaxe I can lend you to finish it off."

"We're not done after the trencher?" John asks, confused. "I thought the trencher was the whole point?"

"Ha, you wish!" Sam laughs back sarcastically. "Yes, in a perfect world, the trencher gets the job done, and there is no hand-digging, but unfortunately, Mike is cheap, and he only bought the trencher with a twelve-inch blade."

"Isn't that good enough?" John asks sincerely.

"Nope, no good. NEC says we need eighteen inches of cover. You know the code book? You're just starting out, but you'll see. You have to go by the code. Everything is in there. You've got ground heave from frost, weight from vehicles, all kinds of stuff. You'll learn. Just keep doing what you're doing," Sam says encouragingly. John sees Steve leaving the barn and knows it's time to get back to it. He pulls his gloves back on and fires the trencher back up, and they finish out their day.

That night, they both get back to their houses exhausted. Between the traffic with the long commute and the digging in the heat, that was a hell of a first day. John sets his empty cooler and thermos on the kitchen table as he makes a beeline for the sink, desperate to get some cold water on his face.

"So," John's mom starts, "how was the first day? You have to tell me all about it."

"It was great!" John replies excitedly. "I'm already learning how to run a trenching machine, and I feel like I'm getting the hang of it. The guys are pretty cool, and the main electrician, Sam, took the time to explain some electrical code stuff to me. He's not licensed yet, but he just finished his hours, and he seems like he knows what he's doing. Those guys work super hard, but I was able to catch him at a good time to learn more about what we were working on. I can't wait to go back tomorrow. I feel like there is a lot for me to learn."

"I'm really proud of you, buddy," John's mom compliments with genuine warmth. "This was all you, kid. You went out there and put your mind to this and created this opportunity for yourself."

Meanwhile, Steve is getting back home at the same time. He comes in with two huge empty jugs of water he bought at a gas station on the way home and wings them into the

CHAPTER 7

recycling bin. "You look beat!" his mom exclaims. "Sit down; I'll get you a glass of water. Tell me all about the first day!"

Steve shrugs and pulls the water glass towards himself, uninterested. "It was okay, I guess. I mean, I don't know. The guys are kind of jerks. I was a little late, but they were giving me a huge attitude about it and really busting my chops. I mean, we're just summer help anyway, who cares?"

"Well, tomorrow is a new day. You get back on it in the morning and show them what you can do," Steve's mom replies, working hard to suppress her frustration with her irresponsible son.

John and Steve both get hired, and things go on like this for a few years. Sam gets his license shortly after the barn job, gets more and more responsibility, and begins to run larger projects. One night, there is an emergency call during a bad storm, and Sam reaches out with a group text.

Sam: Power outage at the school. Who's in boys?? Overtime!

John immediately gives Steve a call, but Steve doesn't seem interested. He had plans with his girlfriend anyway, so he figures he'll catch the next one. John tells his girlfriend he's getting called back in, and she understands. That night, he gets to see Sam navigate a crisis.

The power is out, and the emergency generator is screaming when they get to the school. The rain is driving down, and there is a general feeling of chaos as they try to make sense of what caused the issue. Sam keeps a cool head, and they end up working until 1:00 a.m. but get the problem fixed. That night, Sam offers to buy John dinner at a twenty-four-hour diner as a thank you for his willingness to help in an emergency, and John gets a chance to pick Sam's brain about what is involved in the state licensing process.

Time goes by, and things roll along more or less the same way. Opportunities for night and weekend work come up regularly, but Steve always seems to have an excuse not to come in. John plans his week on Sunday night and preps lunch for the week, but Steve tends to show up unprepared and has to drive to a local deli wherever they're working to buy lunch every day. John is starting to save up a good nest egg from the overtime. He's also saving a ton of money bringing lunch to work since John and Steve still live at home. John shows up at the shop one day with all new power tools. "Must be nice," Steve sneers, embarrassed that his friend is outdoing him.

"Hey, maybe you should take some overtime. Don't be mad at me," John quips as he blows past Steve.

Two years into their tenure with Mike, Sam, and the rest of the crew, everyone starts hearing talk of an economic downturn. People from other companies are being laid off already. There is talk everywhere about how the housing market is slowing down and the commercial market is easing back on new development opportunities. The company is set to start a large project, wiring a shipping center for a trucking company, but they get the news from the builder that the investors are pulling out of the deal.

With that big contract no longer in sight, the boss doesn't have enough work for the entire company, and he's got to make some decisions. He calls Mike and Sam (who now has become one of the lead guys in the company) into a meeting to discuss who should be laid off and who should be kept working. As they run through the roster, they get to John and Steve. Everyone agrees that John is too valuable to lose; there is no way he can be laid off. He's learning very quickly and is extremely reliable. Steve has attendance issues already and sometimes has a poor attitude. Mike remembers a few times he didn't take constructive feedback very well and ended up sneaking out of work early instead of finishing his day. They all agree that John stays and Steve goes.

They break the news to the guys, and John is genuinely sorry for Steve's position. "You'll find a way to stay busy," he assured Steve. "The second this economy rebounds, I'm sure you'll be the first guy they reach out to." Steve has trouble finding electrical work during the layoff. He works for a general contractor, loading dumpsters and delivering material for a few weeks, but that guy is also slow, and the twenty hours he's giving him a week isn't enough for Steve to pay the bills. He gets through the next year doing odd jobs, shoveling snow in the winter and cleaning gutters in the spring.

By the time he gets back to work from his layoff, John is so far ahead of him in his apprenticeship that Steve will never catch up. Before the layoff, Steve had already lost quite a few hours by calling out sick on too many Mondays and cutting out early on too many Fridays. John racked up his hours steadily and never missed a beat except for a week-long trip to the beach with his family every summer. During the slow times, John had more time to ask questions and seek new opportunities. He was able to get some one-on-one time with the boss and asked about how cost estimates were figured on projects. One day a week, the boss let John work a half day in the office, getting familiar with the estimating process and learning a little more about the "behind the scenes" side of the electrical business.

After a brief stint back with the company, Steve tells John he's leaving, complaining that the company never cared about him and has treated him unfairly. John listens with a sympathetic ear, but in his mind, he can't agree with Steve. In his experience, the company has been fair to him. Mike can be hard on people, but you can't take it personally, and he feels like Steve has become bitter about things that were just business decisions. He wishes Steve well with the new company, and they part ways.

A few years later, John is standing at the supply house counter and hears a familiar voice. He turns around to see Steve. He is surprised and happy to see him. They shake hands, and both agree on what a shame it is that they've lost touch over the years. John asks Steve how work is going.

"Well, ya know," Steve nervously shrugs. "Things are going along, I guess. That other company I went to made a lot of false promises, and that really set me back. I should have stuck with you guys after you took me back. It kind of burnt me out from the trade, so I did some carpentry for a while, working for a cabinet-making shop. I'm really looking to get back into electrical now, though, and I'm finally getting serious about it. My wife and I are expecting a kid soon, and I really need to finish my apprenticeship so I can be making journeyman pay. I took a few practice exams to get ready, but I realize how much I don't know, and I keep failing the exams".

John tries to hide his shock at what he's hearing. It's been seven years since that first job he and Steve took digging that trench, and Steve *still* doesn't have his electrical license? John knows that Steve is going to ask about him, and he quickly rehearses in his head how to catch Steve up on things without bragging

He lets Steve know that things went well with the last company and that he was able to get his master electrician's license. Last year, the boss announced his retirement, and John was in a position to buy the company from him.

"Wow, John, good for you," Steve says with admiration. "I had no idea you were a businessman now. That's pretty crazy to hear. You always had better luck than me, though, man. You always seemed to be in the right place at the right

CHAPTER 7

time, but good for you. Anyway, I gotta run. Maybe you can hook me up with a job!" Steve says half-jokingly, feeling out John's reaction.

"I'll see you around, Steve. Good luck, buddy." The two shake hands, and Steve heads out the door. The guy at the supply house counter laughs to himself as the conversation wraps up. He's the same guy that worked there seven years ago, and he remembers the day he introduced those guys to Mike. "You can lead a horse to water, but you can't make him drink," he quips at John as he grabs a cart full of materials.

What can we learn from John and Steve's experience? What are some of the factors that played a role in their successes and failures?

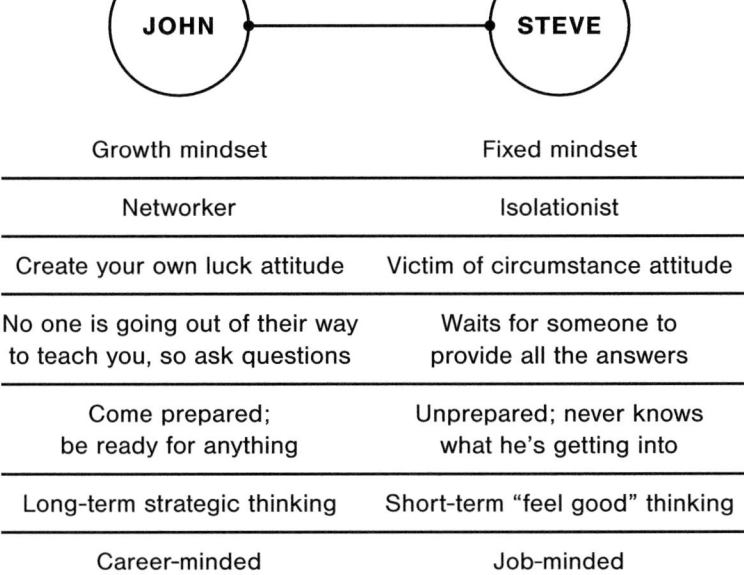

JOHN	STEVE
Growth mindset	Fixed mindset
Networker	Isolationist
Create your own luck attitude	Victim of circumstance attitude
No one is going out of their way to teach you, so ask questions	Waits for someone to provide all the answers
Come prepared; be ready for anything	Unprepared; never knows what he's getting into
Long-term strategic thinking	Short-term "feel good" thinking
Career-minded	Job-minded

One of the unfortunate realities of this world is that your ability to interact with people will determine *some* level of your ultimate success. This is something that I myself have struggled with. I tend to like to work alone and do things my way, sometimes to my detriment. However, if you keep in the back of your mind that successful interactions with others will often produce successful personal results, it becomes a little easier to act on that principle.

For example, John went out of his way to learn a few things from Sam way back on the first day. He didn't know Sam from a stranger any more than Steve did. They had the same opportunity to gain knowledge, yet John took action, and Steve didn't. That one interaction didn't mean much to Sam; in fact, he probably forgot about it by the time he left work that day. However, what it did do was start a conversation and a certain dialogue between a skilled electrician (Sam) and a willing and eager helper (John).

Whether he was conscious of it or not, Sam's next interaction with John might have been a little more pleasant than his next interaction with Steve just because of that sliver of familiarity he gained with John's mentality. In the back of his mind, he might see John as someone who is "all in" on learning, while Steve cares more about taking a break than learning anything. One interaction doesn't mean much in isolation, but the repeated action of proving yourself time and time again will build credibility with your coworkers.

The most important thing is that you walk the walk rather than just talk the talk. For example, if you're asking a lot of intelligent questions, that's a good sign to your supervisor. However, if a year goes by and you're making the same mistakes, you'll lose credibility. Your boss loves your level of interest; you're asking all the right things. The problem is that your technical skills don't seem to be improving. So you're falling short where the rubber meets the road. Good intentions are great, but without a clear focus on the follow-through, you will cap your success.

CHAPTER 7

No one will notice that you were on time to work today, but they may notice that you were on time every day for a year. No one will think much of the fact that you didn't give up on a tough job, but they'll notice that you never gave up on the last ten tough jobs. You start to build a rapport and a reputation for your work ethic, reliability, attention to detail, willingness to learn, mental toughness, or whatever your strengths may be.

Action Items

- ✓ Do you see yourself anywhere in the story or John and Steve? Be honest with yourself if you have some tendencies that are more in common with Steve. Were you aware of them previously? What can you do to improve?

- ✓ Make a list of the three main takeaways from the story.

- ✓ Make a list of five things you'll make sure you do to ensure that you have a successful apprenticeship.

- ✓ What can you do today to set yourself up for success for tomorrow? Do you have a mentor? Can you think of anyone who can function as one?

Chapter 8

Theory Vs. Practice:
The Value Of Hands-On Experience

I'm going to pick on engineers here for a minute. (Sorry, guys! If you're an engineer or dream of becoming one, I respect that. Don't take it personally!) The work of an electrician is a perfect balance of theory and practice. Where they converge is where the magic really happens. Some brilliant engineers can design a complicated system that 99 percent of the population couldn't even dream of comprehending. But those same engineers can't even hang a picture frame or turn a screw without fumbling around.

Some highly skilled electricians can execute the mechanical work like a machine. Their conduit work may look like a robot must have installed it. However, at the first sign of something going wrong, they couldn't troubleshoot to save their lives. These guys may be the best in their respective lanes and might be making a fantastic living for themselves. There is absolutely nothing wrong with sticking with what you know and mastering it. However, the truly skilled electrician is a Renaissance man of the skilled trades. He has a deep understanding of both the national electrical code and electrical theory, but he also has the mechanical ability to masterfully execute the physical work. This is where theory and practice converge to make a truly unique tradesperson and to make you someone who is worth a lot of money in the marketplace.

Let's say a breaker is tripping randomly at a commercial building. An unskilled electrician may grab his tools instinctively and start poking around at almost everything. He might reset the breaker a few times. He might run out to the van to grab a new one. When that doesn't fix the problem, he might ramble some speculative nonsense to the customer to deflect from the fact that he doesn't really know what to look for.

On the other hand, a skilled electrician knows his theory *and* his code. He'll ask intelligent questions. What were you using when the breaker tripped? How often does it trip? Does it seem to coincide with any particular events? For example, does it tend to trip on rainy days rather than dry days? What is the rating of the breaker? Was it adequately sized for the branch circuit wiring and the equipment that it protects?

The skilled electrician understands this convergence between theory and practice and applies his knowledge based on the answers he's getting. He understands the relationship between voltage, current, and resistance because he's familiar with Ohm's law. He knows how to use his meter effectively and which settings to use for testing different applications. He knows which parameters to look for and what they tell him about the nature of the issue. He might immediately perform a resistance test on the wiring or a voltage test on the breaker. Much like a good doctor, he is looking

CHAPTER 8

for the root cause of the issue. A tradesman who just throws parts at a problem with endless trips to the supply house is like a bad doctor who just prescribes an endless string of medications to his patient. Don't be that guy! Learn to truly diagnose issues so that you can move to a resolution.

Of course, this comes from years and years of experience in a multitude of challenging situations. The first few troubleshooting calls you take will feel stressful and overwhelming, but don't worry; we all started like that. Remember that stress and pressure are not always a bad thing. As corny as it sounds, it's true that pressure makes a diamond out of a lump of coal! Remember that you get a little better every time you're in a little over your head. But don't squander those learning opportunities.

Think about how long it took you to solve the problem. If you spent four hours on something a master electrician would have figured out in twenty minutes, you still have a way to go. It's all part of the process, and as long as you're improving, you just need to keep at it until you master it. Psychologists will tell you that it takes ten thousand hours to master something. Connecting what you see in the field to what you're studying in your apprentice classes will unlock a shortcut to that ten-thousand-hour mastery.

So, with this in mind, here are some ways to gain a little more experience and find that balance between theory and practice:

Ride along on an emergency call. Tell your boss you want to assist after hours on a downed power line call or a component failure at a factory. Even if you have to stay out of the way and take more of an assistant role, you'll learn a lot by seeing a senior electrician handle the situation. You'll also have their full attention on the ride back to the shop to interview them on their thought process as they found the problem.

Do some daydreaming in class. What I mean here is to think about real-life practical applications when you're in your theory classes in trade school. E=IR, voltage equals current times resistance, blah, blah, blah. We've all heard Ohm's law a million times. Instead of tuning it out, flashback to a time you saw someone apply it in the field. Maybe you can tie it back to something you saw your boss work on a few weeks ago but didn't quite understand at the time.

What makes a breaker trip? Current. Didn't you overhear your boss say something about high resistance on a pinched wire a few weeks ago? That must have been what was causing that breaker to trip! You may not understand it in the field because you're in a fast-paced, chaotic environment that's not always conducive to learning. But you may also tune it out in class because it sounds so tedious. Finding that intersection between the two is where you'll truly benefit.

Throw yourself into new situations. Now, there's a fine line between taking on a challenge and biting off more than you can chew, and I've tempted fate on way too many jobs like this myself, but shoot for a slightly harder challenge than you think you're ready to handle. Let yourself struggle through something for a little while before calling for help. If you immediately reach for your phone to call your boss the second things get tough, you're not letting yourself build resiliency. You'll start to expect a bailout on everything you don't understand and fail to develop that muscle memory of what it feels like to push through a difficult challenge. When the pressure is on, you'll learn quickly! And most importantly, you won't forget those lessons. So don't be afraid to let yourself get a little lost in a problem as long as you're determined to ultimately solve it.

Don't forget to do your homework. On-the-job experience is the best way to learn any trade. Your tech school classes will

CHAPTER 8

help reinforce that theory and help you build a basic foundation of knowledge. However, the best learning for most people comes with self-study. You might be taking a class at night on motor controls. That's great and could benefit you one day, but let's say you just spent the last eight hours bending conduit. Motor controls are great, and you'll learn them when the time is right, but the school isn't going to tailor its curriculum to your personal experience. That's up to you. If you're really motivated to become better with conduit bending, study that yourself at night. Take a deep dive into some of your textbooks and get into the zone on the theory so you can put it all together. Maybe you can stay late one night after your motor controls class to pick the brain of your instructor or classmates on aspects of conduit bending that you're having trouble understanding.

Find a mentor. (More about this in a minute.) Not everyone is a natural teacher. You might work with a great crew of very talented and knowledgeable licensed electricians, but they may not have any desire to teach you. We're all busy with our own lives. We have families, kids, bills to pay, and all sorts of responsibilities. Not everyone you work with will be as supportive of your interest in the electrical trade.

When you do find someone willing to teach, make sure you respect their time and space. Remember, this guy is not your tutor. Don't follow him around like a stray dog expecting him to reveal all the magic secrets. Learn what you can and ask intelligent questions. Know when to back off when you're slowing down progress or abusing his patience and kindness. I was lucky enough to have a few good mentors along my way, but I made sure to respect their limits. Knowing when it's time to learn and when it's time to shut up and do will go a long way with people.

Also, don't neglect the possibility of having multiple mentors. You can learn from nearly anyone. You might even be able to learn from your fellow apprentices. One of your coworkers may lack the technical knowledge and experience, but he may have the most voracious work ethic you've ever seen. Another coworker might also lack technical skills but be extremely intelligent. Maybe you can pay attention to how he approaches a problem and take a page from his book. Don't discount anyone. People can surprise you.

A Note On Mentors

I'm incredibly thankful to have been blessed with some great mentors in my time in the trade. The funny thing is that most mentors don't even know they're mentors. You may look up to an older electrician and be inspired by him, but he may not even notice. To him, you're just a motivated young person with a desire to learn and a good listening ear. He's just doing his job and may not understand the developmental impact he has on you early in your career.

The mentorship aspect of your electrical journey just reinforces how crucial good relationships and networking are. I've met all my best mentors through simple networking and talking to the right people. I've always made a point to become friendly with the counter salesmen at the supply houses because they get a firsthand look at all the local companies and electricians. Always treat them with respect and develop a good alliance with them. They love to talk and tell you who to hang out with and who to avoid. I've been introduced to people through supply house acquaintances who have become close lifelong friends. It's not only added depth to my personal life but it's boosted my professional life tenfold. Many doors in my life have been opened by simply asking the right questions to the right person at the right time and not being shy about asking for an opportunity.

CHAPTER 8

I once called the number on the side of a truck because I was looking for some extra night and weekend work. They happened to be extremely busy and were hurting for licensed electricians. They asked me if I could come down to their office for an interview, and I said, "Sure, when would you like me there?" They said twenty minutes! The shop was an eighteen-minute drive from my apartment!

I threw on my dress shoes and a polo shirt and flew down there. After a five-minute interview, they hired me on the spot. They asked how much I was looking for as an hourly wage, and I threw out a number. They told me they could do better and upped the offer on their own! I couldn't believe it. That part-time gig to make a few extra dollars became a full-time job, and I stayed with them for a year. I met two amazing mentors at that company who honestly changed the course of my career. I learned more in that year than I ever thought possible and was exposed to interesting electrical work and the business side of electrical contracting. The owner of that company helped put me on a path to entrepreneurship, and I started my own company at the end of my one-year tenure. All because I called the number on the side of a passing electrical truck. You can't make this stuff up, but it does go to show you that networking is critical. I can't stress that enough.

In another situation, I was at a supply house, and another young electrical contractor about my age was describing a recent problem he was having. The guy said, "I don't really know much about that, but I know exactly the right guy to talk to," as he pointed at me. I stepped outside with the electrician and asked how I could help him. He must have been satisfied with my answer because he invited me to meet him at a big job that he wasn't sure he had the capacity to take on by himself. We ended up taking it on as a joint venture and had a great time working together. We stayed in touch for many years after that and passed a lot of business back and forth.

One of my greatest mentors was an older electrician I met at that same supply house. I was grabbing parts for a job, and I ran into an old timer who had known me since I was an apprentice. We were reminiscing about old times and how young I was when the regular supply house guys started to get to know me. (Don't forget I was only seventeen years old when I started full-time in the electrical trade. I was practically still a kid.)

An older electrician overheard this exchange and bragged about how he'd been doing this longer than I'd been alive. At first, I was a little put off by him, but he told me how impressed he was with seeing a young guy who was so serious about the trade. I was twenty-six, and I already had three electrical licenses to my name. On top of that, I was running my own business and expanding by hiring other electricians. He told me he was slowing down as he got closer to retirement and sometimes landed bigger projects he didn't want to take on solo. He invited me to work on a job with him to see if I could be a good "free agent" type of partner to pass leads to and team up with on occasion.

From the first job we did, we hit it off immediately. We've done many jobs together over the years and have become close friends. We worked together the day I met the woman who would become my wife, and he was there years later when we tied the knot. Although now we do more talking than electrical work, we still get together for dinner regularly. He invited me into another electrical organization that promotes continuing education for licensed electricians. I ended up serving as president of that organization for a few years and helped run many professional development classes, which got me noticed by a local trade school teacher and turned into a job at a local technical college. Although I've since stepped down from both positions, I met some amazing people along the way and opened countless doors in my professional life, including a connection to the company where I'm currently employed.

Please don't be afraid to build relationships and seek opportunities. People will help you. They just need you to prove that you're willing to help yourself.

Action Items

- ⊘ Are you more of a book learner or a hands-on learner? How can you turn your learning style into a strength in the electrical trade?

- ⊘ What do you know about the process of troubleshooting? If you've never worked in the electrical industry, have you ever had to troubleshoot a car, a motorcycle, a computer, or a lawnmower? What kinds of steps did you take? What did you learn?

- ⊘ What new situation can you throw yourself into this week that can help you grow?

Chapter 9

Side Jobs: A Dirty Word

I'm going to talk about something very controversial here, but I feel like it's a topic that is seldom discussed openly: SIDE JOBS! I remember vividly, early on in my career, my friend and I both passed the entrance exam for the electrician's union. When we walked out of there, the first thing he said was, "Dude, think of all the side jobs we're going to get!" We hadn't touched a tool or been on a jobsite yet, and this guy was already thinking about side jobs. There are just some people who are natural-born entrepreneurs who can't help themselves. They find ways to maximize their income any way they can, which often means looking for opportunities outside their current employer.

Are side jobs bad? Are you taking work from your boss? Are you breaking the law by doing unlicensed work? Let's talk about the 101 on all things side job. Please note that I am not endorsing side jobs, nor do I want to encourage anyone to do them. The last thing I want is for a bunch of unskilled, unlicensed electricians doing hack work out there, destroying homes and buildings. I am simply acknowledging that side jobs are an inevitable part of the skilled trades world, and this topic will come up in your career sooner or later. When it does, you'll have some background on the ins and outs of it all.

What Are Side Jobs?

Side jobs are also referred to as moonlighting. The term applies to doing any electrical work outside your normal employment for anyone other than your current boss. If you work Monday through Friday but have a small contracting company where you serve your own customers, that's a side job. If you get out of work at 3:00 but help out another company or work on your own until 8:00, that's a side job. If you work for ABC Electric Inc. but your buddy over at XYZ Electric Inc. got you in the door for some night and weekend work, that's a side job.

Are Side Jobs Bad?

Can side jobs be bad? Yes, in certain contexts. Can side jobs be harmless? Absolutely. Your boss may strongly discourage you from doing side jobs. If you agree to his terms and do them anyway, you are not only being dishonest, but you are breaking his trust. There is a right way and a wrong way to do side jobs. I will be the first to admit that I've done TONS of side work in my career. I've even worked a full forty-hour week for a company during the day and a full forty-hour week for a different company on nights and weekends. (That only lasted about three months, and if you wonder why, Google "burnout.")

CHAPTER 9

If you're going to do side work, be a gentleman about it, and don't ruin your reputation. Ninety percent of the people reading this will do it anyway, so here are some general guidelines.

- ⚡ **Am I qualified to do this work?** If you have any inkling that you're in over your head, do not take the work. You can get into a real mess if you take on something you're not qualified for.

- ⚡ **Am I breaking any laws?** If you are an unlicensed apprentice, are you doing work only a licensed electrician should perform? Never do unpermitted work that requires a building permit if you're not prepared and capable of obtaining one.

- ⚡ **Am I stealing work from my boss?** Do not under any circumstances become an undercutter. If you are working on a job, and a customer approaches you to cut out your boss and work for them directly, do not under any circumstances do this. This will soil your reputation and possibly end your career very quickly. Don't bite the hand that feeds. Your boss has overhead. He may need to charge $150 an hour to maintain a team of highly qualified licensed electricians. If you are an unlicensed electrician, performing illegal, unpermitted work for $40 an hour in cash, you will quickly make enemies while you slam doors closed on your career.

- ⚡ **Can I source my own work?** If you feel that you're qualified to do the work and want to start through friends and family, I would say use your best judgment. Again, I am not *encouraging* anyone to do side work. I also don't live under a rock. Start with friends and family. Don't bite off more than you can chew. If something is beyond your level of competence, refer them to a licensed electrician. Remember that if you aren't licensed and insured, anything that goes wrong will cost you one thousand times more than the job will ever pay.

⚡ **Am I going to get into trouble?** If you are a qualified, licensed electrician, your only issue is with your employer. Are you cutting out early to focus on a side job? Are you calling out sick to service your own customers rather than taking care of your primary commitments? Is your mental energy going to your side work, keeping from you having your head in the game during your normal workday? If so, this is a huge problem. However, if you're doing small jobs, it's not affecting your full-time employment, and you're not stealing work from your boss, I say have at it. Remember, if you're taking full-time benefits but only working part-time hours, you're stealing.

⚡ **What if I'm not licensed yet?** Then the chances of you getting in trouble are much higher. Are you an undercutter, taking work from a licensed contractor? You're going to make some enemies in this small circle. Are you doing unpermitted work? If you get caught by the building inspector, this can be extremely problematic for you. Remember, the building inspector, as defined by the National Electrical Code, is the Authority Having Jurisdiction. If you make him mad, he can make your life hell and cost you a lot of money. Are you doing high-liability work? In the state of Connecticut, you need a master electrician's license in order to hold a liability insurance policy. This means that if you are doing unlicensed work, you will NEVER be capable of holding insurance. If something goes awry on a job and you cause a fire, damage a home or building, get busted by the building department, or piss off the wrong guy and get sued, you will have absolutely no leg to stand on in court, and you'll be raked over the coals. This goes back to using good judgment and knowing which jobs you can easily handle and which jobs are over your head. Don't get greedy.

At the end of the day, dirty word or not, we all do side work. I would encourage you to employ your best judgment. Make allies in this trade, not enemies. Choose loyalty over quick cash. Be honest with yourself about your work capacity. We all have different ethics and morals, so I cannot answer what is right for you. I just ask you to be honest with yourself. Don't do anything to hurt the trade that puts food on your table.

Action Items

- How would you handle a situation where a customer was approaching you directly to do work without a license behind your boss' back?

- Have you ever worked a side job with a licensed electrician? Do you know anyone who might be willing to let you ride along with them on a night or weekend shift?

Chapter 10

Staying Organized And Knowing What To Expect

"A clean site is a safe site." You'll hear this so often throughout your electrical career that it will get old. But there is a lot of truth to this, and it doesn't just apply to the jobsite. You can apply this to your personal approach as well. An organized electrician is an effective electrician.

- ⚡ Keep notes throughout the day on your favorite app or simply with a notebook and pencil.

- ⚡ Make material lists throughout the day to give to your supervisor. This will keep the van or the jobsite stocked with everything your guys need.

- ⚡ Give a report to your foreman, superintendent, or project manager at the end of every day. He has a lot to keep track of, so letting him know where you left off will help him set the next level of priorities for tomorrow's schedule.

- Make notes of things you're having trouble understanding. Electrical is almost like learning another language; it takes time to wrap your head around. Keep a list so you can look things up in the codebook after work to better understand what you've seen.

- Do a general review of your day. What did you learn? Are you memorizing the names of common parts? Are you referencing your codebook to build that connection between theory and practice as it applies to the tasks you're performing?

- Keep a log of the different jobs you've done. Maybe it's been a year since you've installed a doorbell system, and you're a little rusty. Luckily, you made a diagram of the last one you did and kept it in your notes to look back on

- Use your smartphone *smartly*. No other generation has ever had Google at their fingertips. You should be a master of quick research, and you should learn to quickly navigate problems and find possible solutions.

- Tool control is important. Keep your toolbox or tool belt neat and organized. Tools are expensive, and losing tools is not only frustrating but it's inefficient. Your most important duty is to show up ready every day to perform the tasks you've been assigned to.

- Materials can get lost very easily on large commercial job sites when there are multiple trades involved and an endless revolving door of delivery trucks. Since you'll likely be the one unloading trucks and sorting materials, keep yourself very organized here. Learn to decipher the packing slip and bill of materials. Document issues with the driver immediately. Once you get the materials off the truck, immediately bring them to the appropriate staging or work area. It's easy for materials to get lost and double-ordered, which wastes time and money on bigger jobs.

⚡ Keeping your van organized is just as much a part of your duties as an electrician as the actual work is because organization facilitates efficiency. Always build time into your weekly schedule to dedicate at least a few minutes to taking inventory and clearing out unnecessary junk. Always return leftover materials because they take up space, and it's just "money on the shelf."

⚡ There are a ton of good productivity apps to keep you organized, and your company may even have some that you're expected to use. Many larger companies use an app called Procore or some variation of it. It is used as a one-stop shop to store all job information and requires you to submit a daily log. I know we like doing electrical work, not paperwork, but remember to carve out the last ten minutes of your day to log your hours, make weekly material lists, and track job status so you're ready when your manager asks for a status update.

A lot of the old timers hate seeing you on your phone, and trust me, there is a lot of validity to that, but remember that your smartphone can be an extremely valuable tool in today's electrical world. Like anything else, don't abuse it, but use it effectively to keep yourself organized, efficient, and ready for anything.

What You'll See In The Residential World

- ⚡ New construction consisting of a lot of running Romex through wood framing.

- ⚡ Remodeling consisting of tracing out old wiring, oftentimes cloth-insulated BX cable, and replacing it with new wiring.

- ⚡ Snaking. Lots and lots of snaking. You'll be catching snakes and wires within walls to fish new wiring in. You may work with many different types of construction, including plaster, plasterboard, and wood or metal lathe. A lot of snaking is done when installing recessed lighting within an existing sheetrock or plaster ceiling.

- ⚡ Service and repair. This will include a lot of troubleshooting of faulty devices and chasing down short circuits and other faults.

- ⚡ If you're in a residential service role, you may deal with a variety of homeowners over the course of a day. You'll run into a lot of different personality types.

- ⚡ Service upgrades, panel swaps, and generator installations, which are common residential projects.

What You'll See In The Commercial World

- ⚡ In new construction, you might wire an entire building from the ground up. You might work with the excavators and the form carpenters in the beginning, laying underground conduit runs for the electrical service and communication utilities. You may see the job all the way through and finish with the final switches and receptacles.

- ⚡ Running conduit. 3/4-inch EMT conduit is the method of choice for much of the commercial industry. You'll become very proficient with measuring, cutting, and bending conduit. Conduits for feeders and services may go up to four inches in diameter, requiring a powered and/or hydraulic bender. Anything over one-and-a-quarter inches is typically not done by hand.

- ⚡ Pulling cable. Depending on where you live, much of your branch circuit wiring may be done in metal clad or MC cable. Individual conductors like THHN can be pulled within conduit runs.

- ⚡ Troubleshooting. Much like residential, you'll chase short circuits and other faults. You may troubleshoot heating and cooling controls, motors, or ethernet cabling in addition to power and lighting

- ⚡ Commercial service work might involve traveling to facilities like restaurants or manufacturing plants to repair devices and systems

- ⚡ Low voltage work. This could cover a wide range of installations, including fire alarm, data cabling, fiber optic, and HVAC controls

What You'll See In The Industrial World

- ⚡ Conduit work. You're probably more likely to run conduit rather than MC cable. You may work in many environments that require rigid metal conduit, which requires the extra work of threading to join runs together.

- ⚡ Motor work. You'll become very proficient with motors in the industrial world as many things throughout our industry depend on them. You'll learn to reverse the rotation, troubleshoot, and start and stop motors. You may work on anything as small as a horsepower blower motor all the way up to a five hundred-horsepower fire pump.

- ⚡ Control wiring. Building off motors, there is a lot of control wiring in the world of the industrial electrician. Motors can utilize customized control circuits that determine when motors start and stop and how they'll relate to other motors and components within a system.

- ⚡ Troubleshooting. This can get more complicated in an industrial setting. You may troubleshoot extensive control cabinets that have involved wiring diagrams. Manufacturing plants are known to have intricate systems that may require constant maintenance and troubleshooting.

Construction Vs Service

Within the plumbing, HVAC, and electrical industries, you'll hear terms and specialties like new construction, remodeling, service work, control wiring, and many others. The trade is roughly split between construction and service. Think of construction as any large project, whether a new skyscraper from the ground up or a complete remodeling of an existing building.

Service relates more to the repair of existing components, systems, and structures.

CHAPTER 10

What You'll See As A Construction Electrician

- ⚡ You may be assigned to the same project for a very long time. It's possible you may report to the same jobsite every day for a year or more.

- ⚡ You may work on a larger crew. A big commercial building may require multiple teams of electricians.

- ⚡ You'll work with others more than you'll work by yourself.

- ⚡ You'll learn what the gang box is and how to take the coffee orders.

- ⚡ You might spend much of your early days organizing the jobsite or taking deliveries from vendors.

- ⚡ You might spend a lot of your time core-drilling concrete floors and walls. Maybe you'll be in a trench for weeks on end, laying conduit for what will become the electrical distribution systems.

- ⚡ You might install and wire a large transformer or panelboard.

- ⚡ You'll be required to operate various equipment and tools, from rotary hammers to scissor lifts, forklifts, and boom lifts.

- ⚡ You may work on the top of a skyscraper tied off with a body harness and lanyard.

- ⚡ You'll learn interesting and specific tasks like exothermic welding and ethernet cabling termination.

Construction electrical work is best for people who like the predictability of going to the same site every day and working the same hours. They might get excited about seeing a large project from start to finish, from the underground utilities to the final light fixtures up in the penthouse suite.

What You'll See As A Service Electrician:

- ⚡ You'll never be on the same job for very long. You might hit multiple job sites in a single day.
- ⚡ You may work on a small team of two while you learn. Once you're licensed, you may work entirely by yourself or get a new apprentice of your own.
- ⚡ You'll learn how to clean up quickly and where every last piece and part is on the van.
- ⚡ You may spend your early days doing supply house runs or simple tasks like putting outlet and switch plates on or hanging light fixtures.
- ⚡ You'll become very proficient at troubleshooting and learn many different electrical systems in-depth.
- ⚡ A given day may take you through power, lighting, communication, and fire alarm systems in an 8-hour shift. Variety is a key part of a service electrician's life.
- ⚡ You will have to think quickly on your feet and learn to make the right call for the situation.
- ⚡ You may get called to an emergency, and you may work unpredictable hours. There is no good "stopping point" with service work. You get to go home when the work is complete or if you get to a stage where it is safe to leave it unattended until tomorrow.
- ⚡ You may wire new circuits, replace motors, work off ladders, or even dig trenches.

CHAPTER 10

⚡ You'll learn interesting, specific things like how to troubleshoot a short circuit, wire access controls to a secure entryway, or trace out an industrial control panel.

Service work is best for people who love challenges and think on their feet. Service work is often very fast-paced, so it might appeal more to energetic people. If you tend to get bored of things easily, the constant variety of service work might help keep you engaged.

Action Items

- ✓ Download a productivity app. Apple and Android both have note apps that can keep you organized, but other apps like Evernote will provide even more features.

- ✓ Practice journaling your workday. What did you work on today? Where were you? What did you learn?

- ✓ Inventory your tools. Do you have everything you need? If not, set some money aside now so you can start to accumulate the necessary tools before you need them. That should include a good multimeter with voltage, amperage, and resistance functions and a non-contact voltage tester.

- ✓ Start learning the names of common parts. Download a catalog from a company whose parts you've seen around, like nVent Caddy or Bridgeport Fittings.

- ✓ Trace out a wiring diagram. Download an automatic transfer switch wiring diagram from Generac or a dimmer switch diagram from Lutron. Trace the lines out and see if you can make sense of it. Can you follow the logic behind the diagram?

- ✓ Buy a copy of the National Electrical Code and the Ugly's Electrical Reference book. You'll need them regardless, so you might as well start now.

Conclusion

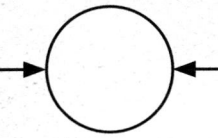

Putting It All Together

Congratulations on making it this far in your journey. If you're serious about the electrical trade, you've just taken the first important step, which is educating yourself. I look forward to sharing this great trade with the next generation of ambitious young men and women who see themselves earning their place in the electrical industry. Remember that there is more opportunity in this field than you can imagine, and it's up to you to put yourself in the right situations. You may find yourself working as a residential electrician or a commercial electrician. You may work new construction jobs or service calls. You might even one day find yourself running your own business as an electrical contractor. You have a long way to go, but the important thing is that you do your research and make strategic decisions that will place you on a good career path. This trade has no shortage of skills to learn and certainly no shortage of challenges. However, I cannot stress enough that it will provide you with a meaningful and lucrative career that you'll look forward to coming back to time and time again, every day, year after year.

I wish you the best of luck on your journey. If you think you have what it takes, I would highly encourage you to enroll in a technical education program and pursue your first job as an electrician's helper. I've included some reference material in the rest of this book that you can return to throughout your next four years as an apprentice. Use this list of skills and actions to assess your journey as you move through the ranks. Are you learning enough? Are you learning at a reasonable pace? Will you be ready for your licensing exams when your big day comes? This can serve as a guide to keep you on track and on pace with the expectations you've set for yourself, as well as the expectations of your employer.

At the end of the day, your level of success is determined by your actions. Work hard, do the right thing, and learn along the way. Always keep your eyes open for an opportunity, and don't shy away from a challenge. This path will take years of dedication and perseverance and will sometimes require some grit and determination. What's waiting at the end is a fun and fulfilling career that will keep you engaged while you earn more and more money over time. If you're not afraid of hard work, what are you waiting for? Start today!

Apprentice Task Checklist

These tasks are based on and organized by chapters of the National Electrical Code (NEC) for clarification and ease of use. By the end of your apprenticeship, it's important that you've had some level of exposure to each task. Some areas you may have mastered, while others may still be foreign to you.

For example, if you've spent your entire apprenticeship with a commercial contractor, you may be well-versed in pipe bending but know nothing about AFCI requirements. Or maybe you've become very proficient with motors but have yet to complete an entire fire alarm system. That's okay because you will gradually gain exposure to all facets of the trade over time. If you know that your company is working on a project with many aspects you're eager to gain experience on, ask your boss to be assigned to that project. Or if an opportunity arises to work nights or weekends, don't hesitate to jump on it. You never know what you might learn.

Use this checklist as a barometer to gauge your experience level. It will put things into perspective and will also help you prepare for your licensing exam, which will be based on the NEC. If you get a fire pump question on your test and you've never even *seen* a fire pump, you may struggle with that question more than someone who can visualize the content.

Chapter 1: General

- Intro to NEC
- AHJ
- Definitions
- Wire terminations
- Working space

Chapter 2: Wiring and Protection

- Neutral conductors – individual
- Neutral conductors – multi-wire branch circuits/shared
- Grounded conductors
- GFCI requirements – residential
- GFCI requirements - commercial
- AFCI requirements – residential

APPRENTICE TASK CHECKLIST

- ◯ Branch circuit requirements – Kitchens
- ◯ Branch circuit requirements – Bathrooms
- ◯ Branch circuit requirements – Living spaces
- ◯ Branch circuit requirements – Garages
- ◯ Ground fault protection for equipment (GFPE)
- ◯ Conductor sizing
- ◯ Continuous vs. noncontinuous loads
- ◯ Over current protection – breaker sizing
- ◯ Outlets vs. receptacles
- ◯ General lighting demands
- ◯ Feeder sizing
- ◯ Appliance wiring – dryers and ranges
- ◯ EV charging stations
- ◯ Services – residential
- ◯ Services – commercial
- ◯ Services – upgrade/replacement
- ◯ Services – panel upgrade/replacement
- ◯ Services – underground
- ◯ Services – disconnecting means
- ◯ Services – conductor sizing
- ◯ Service entrance conductors
- ◯ Overhead service clearances

- Panelboards – MLO vs. MCB
- Main bonding jumpers - location and definitions
- Grounding and bonding – definition and difference
- Grounding electrodes – sizing and permitted electrodes
- Grounding electrode conductors
- Equipment grounding conductors
- Grounding separate buildings
- Supplemental electrodes (ground rods)
- Bonding bushings
- Grounding for parallel raceways
- Transformer grounding and bonding

Chapter 3: Wiring Methods and Materials

- Conductor sizes
- Wires vs. cables
- Protection from physical damage
- Underground installations
- Damp and wet locations
- Framing fundamentals
- Raceway sealing

APPRENTICE TASK CHECKLIST

○ Conductor properties
○ Allowable ampacities
○ Device and pull box sizing
○ MC cable installation
○ NM cable installation
○ PVC conduit installation
○ EMT conduit installation
○ RMC conduit installation
○ LFNC conduit installation
○ LFMC conduit installation
○ Flexible metallic conduit installation
○ Busways
○ Wiremold raceways
○ Knob and tube wiring

Chapter 4: Equipment for General Use

○ Flexible cords
○ Switches – Single pole
○ Switches – Three way
○ Switches – Four way
○ Switches – Motor rated

147

NOT AFRAID TO WORK

- Switches – Smart switches
- Timeclocks
- Dimmers – Wattage ratings
- Dimmers – Compatibility
- Receptacle types
- Receptacle mounting
- Receptacles - Wet locations
- Receptacles – Ungrounded
- Receptacles – GFCI
- Receptacles – AFCI
- Receptacles – Twistlock
- Receptacles – Tamper resistant
- Luminaires – Surface mounted
- Luminaires – Recessed IC
- Luminaires – Recessed non-IC
- Luminaires – LED non-dimming
- Luminaires – LED 0-10V dimming
- Luminaires – Fluorescent
- Luminaires – Exit and emergency
- Ballast replacement
- Electric heat – Calculated load
- Electric heat – Thermostat control

APPRENTICE TASK CHECKLIST

- ○ Electric heat- Deicing circuits
- ○ Motors – Horsepower ratings
- ○ Motors – Disconnecting means
- ○ Motors – Conductor sizing
- ○ Motors – Controllers
- ○ Motors – Overload and thermal protection
- ○ Motors – Reversing rotation
- ○ Motors – Full load current vs. locked rotor current
- ○ HVAC wiring – Condensers
- ○ HVAC wiring – Air handlers
- ○ HVAC wiring – Furnaces
- ○ HVAC wiring – Boilers
- ○ HVAC wiring – Reading nameplates
- ○ HVAC wiring – Thermostat controls
- ○ Doorbell wiring
- ○ Generators – Feeder sizing
- ○ Generators – ATS installation
- ○ Generators – Manual transfer switches
- ○ Generators – Grounding and bonding
- ○ Generators – Portable
- ○ Generators – MCB interlock
- ○ Generators – Emergency sub-panel

- Transformers – kVA ratings
- Transformers – Nominal voltages
- Transformers – Delta vs. wye secondaries
- Transformers – Primary OCPD
- Transformers – Secondary OCPD
- Transformers – Bastard leg services

Chapter 5: Special Occupancies

- Hazardous locations class I
- Hazardous locations class II
- Hazardous locations class III
- Hazardous locations – Seal offs
- Health care facilities – Patient care areas
- Health care facilities – HCF grade wiring
- Marinas and boatyards

APPRENTICE TASK CHECKLIST

Chapter 6: Special Equipment

- ○ EV chargers – Hardwired
- ○ EV chargers – Receptacle
- ○ EV chargers – Disconnecting means
- ○ Swimming pools – Circuits required
- ○ Swimming pools – Timers
- ○ Swimming pools – Heaters/Timers with fireman's switch
- ○ Swimming pools – Equipotential bonding
- ○ Swimming pools – Underwater luminaires
- ○ Swimming pools – GFCI requirements
- ○ Swimming pools – General clearances
- ○ Hot tubs/spas – GFCI requirements
- ○ Hot tubs/spas – Disconnecting means
- ○ PV systems
- ○ Fire pumps

Chapter 7: Special Conditions

- ○ Fire alarm wiring

Chapter 8: Communication Systems

- Cat6 termination
- Coax termination

Service and Troubleshooting

- Dead short
- Intermittent short
- No power at receptacle
- No power at light fixture
- Multimeter – Resistance testing
- Multimeter – Amperage testing
- Multimeter – Voltage testing
- Open neutral
- Three way not working
- Four-way not working
- Arcing on receptacle
- Arcing on breaker
- Storm call (downed powerline with damaged service)
- Control wiring, contactor troubleshooting
- Motor troubleshooting, single-phasing and overheating issues

APPRENTICE TASK CHECKLIST

Soft Skills

○ Dealing with difficult customers

○ Leadership

○ Working in a residential service setting

○ Getting your paperwork done

○ Callbacks

○ Writing up work orders properly

○ Using your resources

○ Communication

Apprenticeship Skill List

Have you been able to get hands-on experience with each of the following items? If you have, rate your level of proficiency and familiarity. If not, ask your boss if you can get in front of each of these items, even if it means staying late or working on a Saturday. Once you get exposure to them, you'll begin to learn that much faster, and your small sacrifice will end up paying dividends. Ask yourself how well you could explain each item to a younger apprentice. What is involved in the installation? What code sections apply to each item?

NOT AFRAID TO WORK

- 👍 Duplex outlet
- 👍 Single pole switch
- 👍 Three way switch
- 👍 Four way switch
- 👍 Old work or remodel box (plaster vs. drywall)
- 👍 New work box
- 👍 Splicing
- 👍 Cable strapping
- 👍 Leaving the correct amount of slack
- 👍 GFCI - Line vs. Load
- 👍 Ohm's Law
- 👍 Taking a continuity reading
- 👍 Taking a voltage reading
- 👍 Taking an amperage reading
- 👍 Testing fuses and breakers
- 👍 Grounding vs. Bonding

APPRENTICESHIP SKILL LIST

- 👍 Single pole breaker
- 👍 Two pole breaker
- 👍 Three pole breaker
- 👍 Shunt trip breaker
- 👍 GFCI breaker
- 👍 AFCI breaker
- 👍 Dual function breaker
- 👍 Identifying hardware - screws, bolts, nuts, washers, etc.
- 👍 Identifying fittings - connectors, couplings, straps, etc.
- 👍 Plaster/mud rings
- 👍 Motor controls and starters
- 👍 Damp and wet locations
- 👍 Outdoor/NEMA3R enclosure
- 👍 Appliance receptacle
- 👍 Hardwired appliances

NOT AFRAID TO WORK

- 👍 A/C disconnect
- 👍 Service riser
- 👍 Service lateral
- 👍 Underground wiring
- 👍 Feeders
- 👍 Copper vs. Aluminum conductors
- 👍 Service cable
- 👍 Meter socket
- 👍 CT meter/cabinet
- 👍 Panel installation
- 👍 Loadcenter vs. Panelboard
- 👍 Sub-panel
- 👍 MC cable
- 👍 NM cable
- 👍 BX cable (cloth insulated)
- 👍 Recessed lighting (old work and new work)

APPRENTICESHIP SKILL LIST

- 👍 Suspended/acoustical ceilings
- 👍 Transformers - control
- 👍 Transformers - distribution
- 👍 Three phase power
- 👍 EMT conduit
- 👍 PVC conduit
- 👍 Rigid conduit (RMC/GRC)
- 👍 EMT bending
- 👍 Photocell controls
- 👍 Timers
- 👍 Ballast replacement
- 👍 Architectural lighting
- 👍 Exterior lighting
- 👍 Bucket truck work
- 👍 Scissor lifts
- 👍 Boom lifts

NOT AFRAID TO WORK

- 👍 Doorbell wiring
- 👍 Thermostat wiring
- 👍 Generator and ATS wiring
- 👍 Exhaust fans
- 👍 HVAC controls
- 👍 Cat6 cabling and termination
- 👍 Fiber optic cabling and termination
- 👍 Snaking wires
- 👍 Rough wiring
- 👍 Core drilling
- 👍 Hammer drilling
- 👍 Trim out
- 👍 Pool wiring
- 👍 Electric heat
- 👍 Firestopping
- 👍 Fire alarm

APPRENTICESHIP SKILL LIST

- 👍 120V smoke and carbon monoxide detectors
- 👍 Reading a tape measure
- 👍 Reading plans
- 👍 Basic customer service
- 👍 Handling a service call
- 👍 Avoiding callbacks
- 👍 Workmanship
- 👍 Work ethic
- 👍 Composure and professional bearing
- 👍 Task planning - making parts lists
- 👍 Basic troubleshooting

Understanding Wiring Diagrams

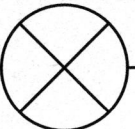

There are several different types of wiring diagrams you'll see throughout your career. They will vary in their level of detail but it's important that you carefully learn to interpret and understand wiring diagrams in all their forms. Think of a wiring diagram as a map. If you follow it in a logical sequence, it should flow through the function of the circuit.

Below is an example of a wiring diagram we would typically refer to as a *one-line diagram*. It represents a general abstract view of the basic functions of a system, but you'll notice it does not go into much detail with exact components within a circuit. Below is a one-line diagram of a typical automatic transfer switch (ATS) for a generator.

Generator Wiring

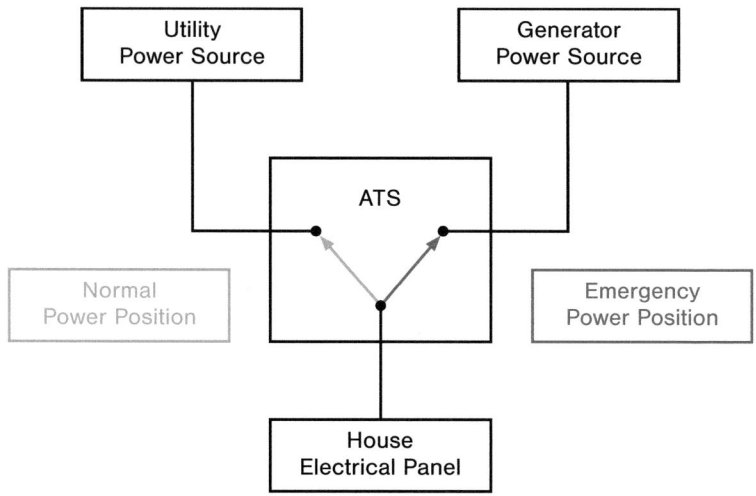

UNDERSTANDING WIRING DIAGRAMS

Other wiring diagrams may go into a higher level of detail, showing each and every component within a system. We sometimes refer to these more detailed diagrams as *schematics*. Below is a typical example of a schematic showing the function of two three-way switches and how they are tied together. Notice the higher level of detail compared to the generator ATS diagram. The internal functions of the switches are shown and individual conductors are highlighted to show the flow of power through the devices.

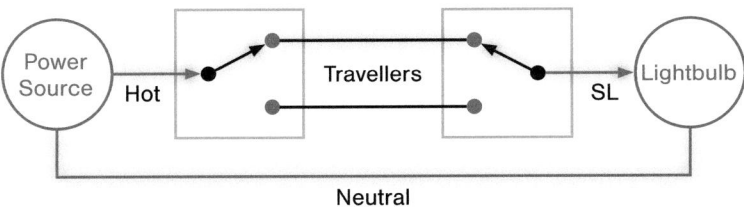

Getting started with wiring diagrams can be like reading another language at first but like anything, practice and careful study will pay you back tenfold throughout your career.

50 Tips
For Apprentices

 Come to work prepared with food and water.

 Don't be afraid to invest in tools. You'll have them for a long time, and having your own tools will make you more efficient.

 Understand there is a hierarchy. You may not agree with the way your foreman wants to do something. You may make a suggestion, but if your suggestion is not well received, shut up and do it his way. Remember, the faster you learn, the faster you can become a lead man or lead woman and run the job how you see fit.

 Always keep a small notebook on you. You'll want to make notes and material lists. If you do it on your phone, your boss will think you're texting or on social media. An old-school notebook and pen is all business.

Anticipate the needs of your journeyman. Know what's next and what you'll need.

 Learn how to load a dumpster effectively so you don't end up with wasted space.

 If you're not busy, jump on cleaning and organization.

 Review your codebook every night. What did you work on that day? Running conduit? Upgrading a service? Read that applicable code section while the task is fresh in your mind to make those connections.

 Don't be afraid to ask questions.

 Dress the part. Work boots, long pants, etc. Have gloves, a hat, whatever else you may need. This includes being prepared for any weather conditions.

 Learn some basic first aid. You're going to cut yourself; it's inevitable. You can't go home for every boo-boo.

 Learn to eat fast.

 Don't argue with your superiors.

Don't bad-mouth other apprentices in front of the boss. One day, you'll be a leader and will be expected to act with integrity. Start practicing now.

 Work on your weaknesses outside of work. Struggling with bending pipe? Practice with some scrap pieces on your own time. You might even want to buy some over the weekend and practice at home.

 Ask for one-on-one training time. Sometimes, the job is fast-paced, and instructional time isn't available.

 Learn a little about each trade. As an electrician, you still need to know how your work interacts with carpenters, plumbers, HVAC, drywallers, etc.

 Work some overtime if needed. When you're young and they need you to stay late, do it.

 Jump on an emergency call. Ride along with a veteran electrician to assist. You'll get to see how someone handles a high-pressure situation where you need to be quick on your feet.

 Build a rapport with the other trades on the site. We all need to work together. Remember, we're on the same team. At the end of the day, we are all there to get the project built.

Don't be too hard on yourself. You're going to make mistakes early on. It's all in the recovery.

 Learn all the different parts. If you're waiting at the supply house, grab a catalog. Or bookmark some common manufacturers you tend to work with on your internet browser.

 Get good at taking coffee orders.

 Find a role model.

 Keep a dust mask in your bag. This one is seriously overlooked. You'll thank me when you spend half your day hammer drilling or saw cutting! Or if you have to go into a filthy crawlspace!

 Don't be afraid to get dirty.

 Embrace new challenges. See setbacks as opportunities.

 Learn about nutrition and stop drinking energy drinks. No one likes a sluggish apprentice who needs his next fix.

 Never fall asleep in a van between jobs.

 Get plenty of rest at night.

Seek out opportunities to learn how to use every tool and every piece of equipment.

 Learn trade slang. A lot of common parts are not called by their official names.

 Have a sense of humor. You'll get picked on, but we all did, and we're still here.

 Learn some leadership skills along the way.

 Never do unauthorized extra work for a customer. Even if a GC or customer pressures you, just tell them you can't make that decision, and it has to go through your supervisor.

 Practice good tool accountability. It's very easy for tools to get lost on jobs. Take some time at the end of the day to gather everything and account for it.

 Slow is smooth, and smooth is fast. Don't try to rush through things when you're frustrated.

 Try not to jump ship from a contractor during your apprenticeship. When times are tough, you can be laid off and lose a lot of time on your apprenticeship hours. If your company is keeping you busy, keep getting your hours in. If you don't see a future there, you can always make a change after you get your license.

NOT AFRAID TO WORK

 Stay positive. Negative talk leads to negative thoughts and actions.

 Keep all the batteries for the cordless tools charged up. Plug the scissor lifts in overnight before you leave for the day.

 Keep a knife on you. You'll constantly be skinning wires, opening boxes, cutting drywall, etc.

 Keep a non-contact voltage tester (volt pen) on you ALL THE TIME. It's extremely important you're able to tell if a circuit is safe at any given time.

 Always test your multimeter on continuity before doing a voltage check. This will tell you that the battery is working properly.

 Move with a sense of purpose. This means you need to keep your energy levels up and make sure you hustle.

 Never waste a trip to the van. Always ask the other guys if they need anything. If someone is done with something, pack it back up on your way back to the van to save on cleanup at the end of the day.

Learn electrical theory. Following orders is one thing, but truly understanding the theory of how electricity flows and how circuits work will take you from being a decent electrician to being an exceptional one.

 Invest in some good knee pads. If you ever have to spend a day installing outlets or floor boxes, your knees will thank you.

 Don't buy cheap tools. Buy good stuff and take care of it.

 Don't neglect low-voltage work. Most guys in the trade gravitate towards power and lighting (120V and above), but learning fire alarm, access controls, data terminations, fiber optic, and HVAC controls will greatly set you apart from the average joe.

 Most importantly, have fun and enjoy the trade! It's a great privilege, and you should be thankful for any opportunity you can find. Embrace it.

 BONUS TIP: Don't fall into the tough guy trap. Don't be the guy who thinks it's cool to sleep for four hours and live off of Monster energy drinks. That guy looks terrible and feels terrible. It's not cool. What's cool is getting proper sleep, eating and exercising properly, and showing up ready to crush the day.

General Knowledge Check

- Is an electric heater a resistive load or a reactive load?

- What is an equipment grounding conductor?

- Can you run EMT outside? If so, under what conditions?

- What does turns ratio refer to?

- What size nut driver do you use on a ground screw?

- How much thread protrusion do you need to show on the end of a bolt going through a tapped hole?

- Explain what a switch loop is.

- Explain the difference between a 2700K lamp and a 4000K lamp. What does K stand for?

GENERAL KNOWLEDGE CHECK

- How many outlets are required for a 60" kitchen countertop section?

- What is the burial depth for a 20A circuit run in PVC conduit?

- Name one situation where you would bond the ground and neutral within a panel and one where you would not bond them together.

- How far do service entrance conductors have to be from a window?

- What kind of load does the neutral in a multiwire branch circuit carry?

- What is the difference between SER cable and SEU cable?

- What does the 'B' in NM-B cable stand for?

- Which of the following requires GFCI protection:
    a) Garbage disposal
    b) Dishwasher
    c) Both a and b

- What is the general rule when placing residential smoke detectors?

GENERAL KNOWLEDGE CHECK

- When is the use of a bonding bushing required?

- What is the difference between grounding and bonding?

- An LED light consists of what two main parts?

- When installing an appliance cord on a 240V dryer or range, when is it appropriate to remove the bonding jumper, and when should it be left in place?

Key Terms

A–Z

Ampacity. The current, in amperes, that a conductor can carry continuously under the conditions of use without exceeding its temperature rating.

Authority Having Jurisdiction (AHJ). An organization, office, or individual responsible for enforcing the requirements of a code or standard or for approving equipment, materials, an installation, or a procedure.

Bonded (Bonding). Connected to establish electrical continuity and conductivity.

Branch Circuit. The circuit conductors between the final overcurrent device protecting the circuit and the outlet(s).

Branch-Circuit Overcurrent Device. A device capable of providing protection for service, feeder, and branch circuits and equipment over the full range of overcurrents between its rated current and its interrupting rating. Branch-circuit overcurrent protective devices are provided with interrupting ratings appropriate for the intended use but no less than 5,000 amperes.

Circuit Breaker. A device designed to open and close a circuit by nonautomatic means and to open the circuit automatically on a predetermined overcurrent without damage to itself when properly applied within its rating.

Conductor, Insulated. A conductor encased within material of composition and thickness that is recognized by this Code as electrical insulation.

Disconnecting Means. A device, or group of devices, or other means by which the conductors of a circuit can be disconnected from their source of supply.

Electric Power Production and Distribution Network. Power production, distribution, and utilization equipment and facilities, such as electric utility systems that deliver electric power to the connected loads, that are external to and not controlled by an interactive system.

Energized. Electrically connected to, or is, a source of voltage.

Feeder. All circuit conductors between the service equipment, the source of a separately derived system or other power supply source, and the final branch-circuit overcurrent device.

Fuse. An overcurrent protective device with a circuit opening fusible part that is heated and severed by the passage of overcurrent through it.

Ground. The earth.

Grounded. (Grounding). Connected (connecting) to ground or to a conductive body that extends the ground connection.

Grounded Conductor. A system or circuit conductor that is intentionally grounded.

KEY TERMS

Grounding Electrode. A conducting object through which a direct connection to earth is established.

Grounding Electrode Conductor. A conductor used to connect the system grounded conductor or the equipment to a grounding electrode or to a point on the grounding electrode system.

Ground-Fault Circuit Interrupter (GFCI). A device intended for the protection of personnel that functions to de-energize a circuit or portion thereof within an established period of time when a current to ground exceeds the values established for a Class A device.

Interrupting Rating. The highest current at rated voltage that a device is intended to interrupt under standard test conditions.

Lighting Outlet. An outlet intended for the direct connection of a lampholder or luminaire.

Metal-Enclosed Power Switchgear. A switchgear assembly completely enclosed on all sides and top with sheet metal (except for ventilating openings and inspection windows) and containing primary power circuit switching, interrupting devices, or both, with buses and connections. The assembly may include control and auxiliary devices. Access to the interior of the enclosure is provided by doors, removable covers, or both. Metal-enclosed power switch gear is available in non-arc-resistant or arc-resistant constructions.

Neutral Conductor. The conductor connected to the neutral point of a system that is intended to carry current under normal conditions.

Overcurrent. Any current in excess of the rated current of equipment or the ampacity of a conductor. It may result from overload, short circuit, or ground fault.

Solar Photovoltaic System. The total components and subsystems that, in combination, convert solar energy into electric energy suitable for connection to a utilization load.

Surge-Protective Device (SPD). A protective device for limiting transient voltages by diverting or limiting surge current

Switch, General-Use. A switch intended for use in general distribution and branch circuits. It is rated in amperes, and it is capable of interrupting its rated current at its rated voltage.

Thermal Protector (as applied to motors). A protective device for assembly as an integral part of a motor or motor compressor that, when properly applied, protects the motor against dangerous overheating due to overload and failure to start.

Voltage (of a circuit). The greatest root-mean-square (rms) (effective) difference of potential between any two conductors of the circuit concerned.

Voltage to Ground. For grounded circuits, the voltage between the given conductor and that point or conductor of the circuit that is grounded; for ungrounded circuits, the greatest voltage between the given conductor and any other conductor of the circuit.

Printed by Libri Plureos GmbH in Hamburg, Germany